The Language of Value

The Language of Value

Solutions for Business Using New Information-Based Currencies

Virginia B. Robertson

BEP

BUSINESS EXPERT PRESS

Leader in applied, concise business books

The Language of Value:
Solutions for Business Using New Information-Based Currencies

First published in 2022 by
Business Expert Press, LLC
222 East 46th Street, New York, NY 10017
www.businessexpertpress.com

ISBN-13: 978-1-63742-179-6 (paperback)
ISBN-13: 978-1-63742-180-2 (e-book)

Business Expert Press Economics and Public Policy Collection

Collection ISSN: 2163-761X (print)
Collection ISSN: 2163-7628 (electronic)

First edition: 2022

10 9 8 7 6 5 4 3 2 1

This book is dedicated to Carol for believing,
to Jordan for seeing,
and to Nick for experiencing.

Description

The world is on the precipice of a transition from dollars to a new type of Information Currency based on the tokenization of Value on the blockchain. Robertson discusses why this transition is happening and how business and government can specifically adapt by using this technology and by learning a new Value language. This book documents these new technologies that provide for sovereignty over your money, sovereignty over the Value of your work, and technologies that secure sovereignty for the Value of your company. This sovereignty includes the ability to freely move Value, store Value, and determine Value. If this resonates with you, then you must read this book. It shows how to implement new cutting-edge technologies of Value to enhance business practices across a wide spectrum of industries.

Keywords

cryptocurrency; blockchain; token; NFT; CPI; bitcoin; ethereum; Web3; IOT; DXY; PPP; supply chain; information currency; item banc; reserve currency; central bank; oracles; IPFS; barter; identity; javascript; great depression; recession; LOOP; decentralized finance; deFi; layer 2; AMM; ERC-20; comparables; blockchain consulting; inflation; metaverse; greatest deception; DEX; decentralized exchange; tokenization; BHN; basic human needs; Value; Language of Value; item bank; commodities; itembanc; chainlink; crypto.com; metamask; uniswap; 1inch; cardano; boson protocol; solana; immutableX; avalanche; moralis; ocean protocol; polygon; Aave; ENS; unstoppable domains; polkadot; rarible; bondly; paid; nexo; coin gecko; bitpay; uphold; morpheus; origin trail; nexus mutual; item banc index

Contents

Testimonials

"The Language of Value *is an extremely timely addition to our thinking at this time. For decades, we have had a very rigid view of the monetary system—Central Banks create a fiat monetary base, then commercial banks multiply this base through the fractional reserve system. The value of everything is measured in fiat currency terms. The invention of digital assets challenges this by suggesting that nongovernment actors can create money, a truly radical idea. Virginia adds to this challenge by suggesting that fiat money as a measure of value of basic items necessary to live is not fit-for-purpose and can be superseded by comparing the value of basic items with each other. Virginia's book also reminds us that barter on a large scale is NOW possible WITH NEW TECHNOLOGIES—effectively bypassing the use of fiat money in the system. These notions challenge the established orthodoxy and may lead us to some unexpected conclusions."*—**Dr. Andrew S. Nevin, PhD, Partner— West Africa Financial Services Leader and Chief Economist, Nigeria Clients and Markets Leader**

"*This book,* The Language of Value, *provides a good introduction to the entire field of cryptocurrencies. It is up-to-date and includes a basic discussion of all relevant topics related to bitcoin and altcoins. Individuals reading the book should see how becoming involved in this emerging field can add value to an organization's bottom line. It's well written and flows smoothly from one topic to the other. The book's author has been studying and investing in cryptocurrencies herself for several years. I myself have been studying and investing in the cryptocurrency sphere since 2016 and am familiar with just about all the concepts in the book. However, the author integrated all relevant concepts and tied them together into a cohesive whole such that I learned much from the book. I plan to utilize the book as a frequent reference whenever I encounter a topic I am not familiar with. The author obviously knows what she is* talking about. *This book should be required reading for all mid-level and upper-level executives, as well as individuals entering the cryptocurrency field for the first time.*"—**Dr. Michael J. Cerullo, Emeritus Professor in the School of Accountancy**

"*It has always been clear to me that Modern Trade/Barter systems exist as a result of the deficiencies of national currencies, but I didn't think of those deficiencies as a lack of 'information' until I met Virginia Robertson and became familiar with the ideas behind (the) Item Banc. In this book, Virginia accurately describes direct trade and the multitude of organized trade/barter systems. They act as easy to understand examples of information currencies that substantiate her vision for information as value and a basis for more equitable currencies.*"—**Annette Riggs, Chairman of the Board, IRTA (International Reciprocal Trade Association)**

"*Wow,* The Language of Value: Solutions for Business Using New Information-Based Currencies *is definitely a valuable read. I wanted to review the content but was slow to start. After I opened the first page, I was quite taken back by the robust amount of information in compact and easy to comprehend format. I can give this to anyone coming into fintech to learn basics to save them quite a lot of heartache. But, as someone in blockchain for 6 years, I felt personally challenged to ponder the technology I'm producing as Ms. Robertson discussed how and why the value of fiat was lost during the Great Depression, the Great Recession, what she states we are experiencing now: the Greatest Deception. You'll want to pick up this fantastic read for a historical outlook and an overall understanding of value and how cutting-edge technologies are changing definitions and regulations found in the financial world. This is truly an incredible amount of knowledge. Thank you for sharing this, I feel it will help a lot of people on this mission to wealth and security.*"—**Alyze Sam, Co-Host, Crypto Couch Podcast, Author,** *Complete Stablecoin Guide 2020,* **MIT Computer Science**

Preface

The Language of Value

Critical Thinking About Monetary Change and the Development of Information Currencies

Everyone is talking about blockchain and cryptocurrencies such as Bitcoin. These technologies represent *Value*, but how will they affect the way we do business? How can executives use these new tools to actually solve business problems? This book provides a functional review of these new technologies and how they can be applied.

I have been working with global trade, blockchain, and cryptocurrencies for several years and know that these technologies will support an information-based currency, or "Information Currency."

This book will show how information about the relative Value of real-world items and services and the technology to transfer this is currency itself, and in addition, technology now exists to digitally represent all physical items and services of Value as capital for transfer and for financial services. The history of this proposal in practice is reviewed and explained in depth.

Information Currency in its current form is harnessing Value data, capitalizing business, and providing doorways into the new decentralized finance (DeFi) frontier. This new Value language is setting up to manage the unique business challenges of our era. If you are a business person, this book will position you in the sea of it.

Readers will learn about:

- Why we need a new language of Value for currencies
- What is a Value language translator for information currency, and how it works
- How relative Value relates to currency, and why it matters
- The role of Item Banc technology
- How we implement a new language of bedrock common Value represented by Value information of Basic Human Needs

- The ability to enter into the new DeFi space using information currency techniques for business Valuation protocol
- A Five-Step Implementation Plan for companies to capitalize their Value with information currency
- How to get management buy-in and employee support
- How to choose information currency applications in business transactions and what key technology and training companies will need
- Real-life examples such as how Marriott solved its cash flow problem
- When will companies need an outside currency consultant
- Reviews of related currency technology products for business

I have designed this book to be useful for corporate executives, students in MBA and MIS programs, executives in professional education programs and seminars, digital currency implementation teams in government, community managers, blockchain communities and thought leaders, finance leaders, and economists.

We are poised to enter an unfamiliar new world of business based on a new Language of Value. This book will help readers align with the changes that are coming and explains how to harness the new currency tools for their business.

—Virginia Robertson
Savannah, Georgia
November, 2021

Your Road Map: How to Use This Book

Economics and cryptocurrencies can be complicated topics. So this book spends a lot of time introducing you to what may be new and technical subjects.

Before you get to the "good stuff"—how to actually start using cryptocurrencies—you've got to have a solid background:

Chapter 1 will give you a good general overview of the book. It explains what a Value language is, why it matters, and why we desperately need a new one.

Chapter 2 discusses how we can devise a new Value language.

Chapter 3 explains the technologies that will power this new Value language, what information currencies are and how they work.

Chapter 4 explores how countries and individuals will make the switch to cryptocurrencies.

Chapter 5 details information currency applications for business, and how we can learn from the practice of barter.

And Chapter 6 explains the Five First Steps you can take toward using cryptocurrencies—how to get involved.

The remaining chapters cover:

When you need an outside currency consultant (Chapter 7).

Specific information currency products for business (Chapter 8).

Steps your business can take to implement information currency (Chapter 9), and

Other important issues: converting information about assets into currency, using industry pools, and a conclusion (Chapter 10, 11).

Introduction

Why Is This Book Relevant?

Companies, people, and countries are converting their dollars to new stores of Value, such as Bitcoin, and are using new technologies for exchange without money by using "directly tokenized Value"—this means that Value is symbolized by a token. The token has Value because it is representative of work that will be or has been performed to give it Value. A token can also represent a claim to an asset. This book can help executives understand what this development means and recommends specific business methods to implement these new technologies. This book is mission-critical to suit up for incoming changes in business currency language, or what this author calls "Value language" worldwide.

We are living through a paradigm shift where new forms of encrypted currency are being escorted deep into our financial worlds. The idea that a technology of money can create and hold Value is confusing and this book explains its context in business so that executives can be prepared.

The long-established pattern in business of transacting exclusively in nation-state-issued currency such as dollars is becoming unsustainable. We may soon see Value based on dollars drowned in inflation because governments allowed the creation of significant amounts of new dollars. We can anticipate this based on the classic economic theory of supply and demand where excess supply of dollars chasing a fixed amount or fewer goods creates price inflation. This developing situation in the world is considered in the urgency of the subject of this book.

The book documents new technologies that provide for sovereignty over your money, sovereignty over the Value of your work, and technologies that secure sovereignty for the Value of your company. This sovereignty includes the ability to freely move Value, store Value, and determine Value.

If this resonates with you, then you must read this book. It will show how to implement new cutting-edge technologies to enhance business practices across a wide spectrum of industries.

CHAPTER 1

Book Overview

A Value Language Translator for Information Currency

Converting Value to Currency

Definitions

The concepts of Value language and information currency can seem complicated, so let's first define some basic terms to make the concepts easy to understand.

In this book the term "Information Currency" is based on an idea: that currency is information, and information is currency. With free information, we can operate with real-time flow of market Value data, such as how much coffee is available in New York versus how much tea is in this same city. To define this further, Information Currency is defined as what is available, where it is available, and at what (relative) Value. The term Information Currency refers to Value transfers that use a new generation of encrypted, automatic contracts that move synthetic representations of assets in secure transactions between sovereign entities. These entities include individuals, companies, and nation states. The entities also already include robots and machines.

The term "Value" is strategically capitalized in this context to represent a philosophical and economic shift that is now upon us. Value will be discussed as real on its own, independent of the dollar-method of exchange. Value has been defined by dollars, but in this book I will explain how it will not be defined exclusively with dollars in our future.

In this text, "dollars" represent any fiat currency (a currency without a backing or standard like the U.S. dollar [USD], the Peso, and the Euro). Dollars operate as a medium of exchange but also as a medium of Value.

This book explains how dollars have become an interruption of direct Value information and Value transfer, or Information Currency.

This book discusses the integration of a technology called "blockchain" as a component of Value discovery—the process that records, secures and reveals Value to the user of information currency.

A blockchain is a digital ledger that records transactions both chronologically and publicly. Blockchains are the underlying technology that power cryptocurrencies and other crypto technologies. Blockchains are powered by "nodes"—which are servers, computers, and other end-point machines hosting and processing transactions of the ledger. Transactions are grouped into "blocks," and the chain of these is what gives the technology its name.[1]

Blockchain is a technology that permanently records a sequence of information items (ledger transactions) secured by encryption between each new set of data transactions. In the context of this book, the ability of blockchains to secure public record of accounts is shown to be fantastically powerful—enough to influence Value as it is possible to have a record of every item in the world, and every service, and every related action, and every entity who participated in an action on a public, discoverable network. This will be shown in this book to ultimately allow each item and service to interact with each other as a Value item instead of needing to pass through some kind of "dollar" to discover its Value.

This book also discusses a new technology called "Item Banc," which is a new technology method to translate items into a measure of Value understood everywhere in the world using a "banc" of commodity item prices around the world as a base to compare Value. This information is super Valuable to businesses in an environment where Value becomes difficult to ascertain for transactions and asset Value assignments. In a market where the dollar price of lumber suddenly doubles, the participants in the market need to know if their assets in dollars should double as well. The technology that addresses this is detailed in later chapters.

In this book, the terms "trade" and "barter" are used interchangeably. The terms "trade" and "barter" are also used to refer to transactions that may include more than two parties. But these archaic-sounding transactions are now coming back, transformed into new, dynamic technologies that have the potential to make dollars, and the institutions that singularly back them, crumble to insignificant Value dust.

Why Value Matters Now

We are experiencing a Value crisis and a Value opportunity at the same time

Value was lost during the Great Depression (1929–1939). Value was lost in the Great Recession (2007–2009). Value is being lost again in what we can call the Greatest Deception—which has actually been going on for some time.

Value is destroyed in cycles by our traditional money system. These cycles are not accidents. We allow institutions to create and assign our Value to their Value, the dollar. The dollar structure destroys Value when we are at the bottom of the financial cycle (during a recession or depression). The dollar's financial structure is designed to expand and contract through financial markets. The Value of the capital in your business is forced to reconcile with dollar allocations. Dollars lose Value from the effect of Central Bank actions that have flooded the money supply and artificially inflated the Value of financial instruments such as derivatives that are not strong or balanced investments across society. For example, the Federal Reserve inflates the money supply by buying treasury securities and corporate bonds from companies (and some of these with a continuing negative price-to-earning ratio). These purchases tend to increase the reserves in the banking system for banks to loan out, and this is how dollars are created. The Federal Reserve can also lower the reserve requirements for banks, as was done on March 26, 2020 when they were lowered to zero.

With the dollar structure, it is also difficult for Value to move. The velocity of money, specifically how fast it changes hands, depends directly on the process to get it and the means to hold it and the method to send it. When we get Value in dollars then banks tell us how to store it, what Value their records say that we have, when we can get it, what form we can get it in, and where we are allowed to send it. This book will explain new technologies where banks do not need to be in the middle, where records of transactions are made permanent during the transaction, where holding Value and investing can happen simultaneously, and where asset Value can be designated, named, and sent anywhere in the world anytime. Value matters now because we are ready and able to make it and move it now.

Value matters now more than ever because for the first time in history we have the technology to secure Value—namely, we can permanently record Value on the blockchain. New technologies of money will redefine the Value of your business and its capital allocation independently of the dollar. Exactly how these technologies can protect and resurrect Value is explained later in this book.

The Role of an Item Banc to Compare Value

In order to move away from dollar Value thinking, we need to adopt a new Value language

The USD has been the global reserve currency. This means that it is the currency used to pay for most international trades, and for important items such as oil. Dollar currency is "reserved" by banks for these payments and for foreign exchange, and has been the base used to translate Value to the world. Due to changes in the global economy and the excessive emergency creation of USD and other national currencies, the old Value benchmarks have changed. The conversion rates of USD to other currencies are in question and the stability of the dollar is weakening (for example, the DXY Index—a measure of the Value of the USD relative to the Value of a basket of currencies of most of the U.S.'s most significant trading partners—has made precipitous falls). This is hard to believe when USD has been so central to Value security for so long. But the dollar index (the DXY chart of the Value of the dollar against a basket of currencies) continues to weaken as the Federal Reserve continues to create more dollars.

The role of Item Banc technology is to offer a new way to compare Value of currency by creating a common Value base. This base can be used to translate dollar Value in one country to the dollar Value in another, creating a currency conversion rate that exists outside of dollar financial markets. Item Banc indexing can also be used for conversion ratios of crypto and other digital currencies. The Item Banc Index derives a Value base by comparing the real-time relative prices of basic human need (BHN) items

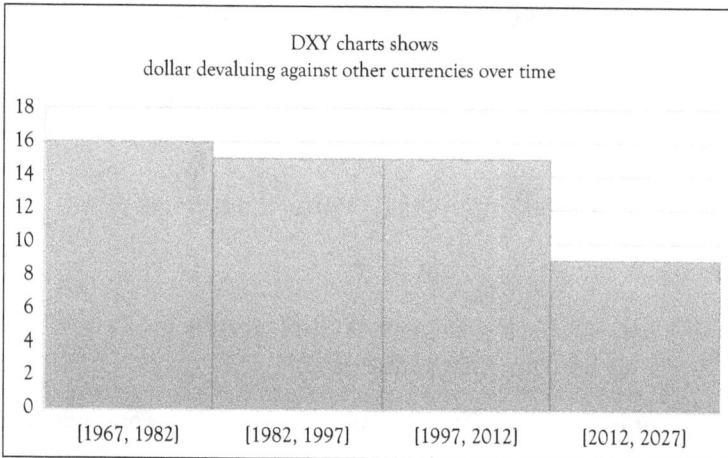

Figure 1.1 DXY index https://tradingview.com/symbols/TVC-DXY/

Source: Robertson 2021

around the world. BHN items might include staple items such as rice, bottled water, shirts, or soap.

In addition to its use for currency conversion, Item Banc Indexing can function as a protocol to cross-Value assets (such as physical things) directly. This is accomplished by computing what are called comparables.

Example: Computing Comparables for Decentralized Finance

Comparables are Values of similar assets used traditionally in real estate finance to compare a similar property with a known or last Value to one that needs Valuation

In the new Information Currency, financial transactions such as loans against assets are executed by automated contracts (smart contracts). These financial transactions function without a bank, or centralized entity in the middle, and so this type of transaction is named "Decentralized Finance" (DeFi). The automated finance contracts need Value information about the asset for which will be used to collateralize a loan. The smart contract can use this information about similar assets, or comparables, to determine a Value against which to grant a loan.

In a similar way, Item Banc technology creates comparables that work across different countries, languages, and currencies all over the world.

These Value comparables are necessary to enable transactions based purely on the Information Currency about what is available where and at what comparable (relative) Value.

Our Languishing Value Language

Definitions

A Value language is a learned pattern of recognizing the relative Value of commonly used products and services

In this century, we primarily understand the relative Value of goods based on a dollar medium of exchange. (As per prior definitions, the "dollar" is used to refer generically to any national currency.)

For example, if a carton of a dozen eggs is two USD and a box of cereal is four USD, then the relative Value of eggs to cereal is one carton of eggs to two boxes of cereal. Yet our language of Value does not compare eggs to cereal. We compare eggs to dollars and cereal to dollars, then dollars to dollars to arrive at a ratio of relative Value.

Our language of Value gets curtailed when we travel to a different country and see items priced in a different kind of dollar. For example, the same carton of eggs in Jamaica is priced at 200 Jamaican dollars (JMD). Since most of us speak a Value language of dollar in the middle or medium of exchange, (as in some kind of dollar or Euro or peso), we are immediately unable to understand what Value 200 means in regard to the price of eggs in Jamaica, in this example. We need to look up a foreign exchange index to convert USD to JMD to get some idea of relative Value. The exchange index becomes a Value translator, or interpreter of our dollar Value language. The Item Banc index offers an alternative method to compare relative dollar Values.

Without a form of dollar in the middle of a transaction between a buyer and a seller, a transaction is more like barter where goods are directly Valued to goods. An expert on barter, the President of Active International (see https://activeinternational.com) in New York, stated to me personally that in his experience, executives in training take a year and a half to adjust to a barter way of Value thinking. In short, a paraphrase of this statement is that it takes this long to naturally transition into a new

Value language. Most people are stuck with a singular dollar language that interferes with direct Value discovery.

Why is dollar Value suddenly a discussion? Dollar language has been the Value language that most of us have spoken for as long as we have lived. But dollar Value language is destroying our civilization. Part of the reason for this is that people do not realize how they have been deceived. When central banks around the world create dollars, your dollars are worth less. The devaluing of our dollars has happened over nearly 50 years and we have become normalized with a narrative that this is allowed and that this is somehow good for us. Why are most people around the world living with this Value deception? Most people in the world do not even know how dollars are created and that for almost 50 years they have been deceived about the Value of dollars, and so it must be named the Greatest Deception. How this has happened exactly will be explained in the following chapters.

New Problems With Our Current Value Languages

Almost every individual speaks the language of Value of his or her national currency. When we see prices in another currency, the Values feel meaningless. We can apply the current currency pair exchange (based on international exchanges) to discover a mathematical conversion but indeed we need to translate back to our own Value language to assess Value. Our Value language is limited to a pairing of goods and services to dollars, where dollars are the only Value translator instead of goods being compared directly to goods or goods directly to services. In addition, our native dollar Value language does not operate on a common base of Value with other national currencies in the world.

The Greatest Deception has been going on for almost 50 years since it began in the early 1970s. This was when we let go of a base of Value for dollars. The base of Value prior to this was gold (backing each dollar was a dollar's worth of physical gold). We had an equivalent Value stored away (in the Fort Knox Bullion depository, for example) and for every dollar created the world could at least compare a USD to the Value of this gold. When President Nixon took America's dollars off the gold standard, the world moved away from gold Value language and into dollar Value language. Soon after, dollars were created from nothing, backed by nothing—the dollar became what is called a fiat currency—and people were deceived into believing that a dollar Value stayed the same and that groceries, cars, and houses were increasing in Value, and not that the dollar was losing Value. This was the Greatest Deception.

Central banks around the world "printed" their own national dollars at will. As a result, we created an irrational Value language that caused painful and destructive recessions that like waves would wipe out the Value of entire societies and their work. The exchange rates of national currencies became equally irrational as the sale of oil was restricted to USD. These dollar exchanges were not able to account for various industries across the world and how their products compared, or basic labor and how it was Valued. Some countries tried to fix the wrong problem with unions or minimum wage laws or scant financial regulations. These Band-Aids still have not stopped the Greatest Deception. It continues.

The world has two challenges from the Greatest Deception that can be fixed. When these challenges are overcome, the world will be able to use a completely new Value language. The first fix will remove the need for a dollar medium of exchange. Dollars are not required to transact Value. A second fix will enable information of a comparable base of Value for transactions.

Why We Need a New Language

We need a new Value language because our currency today is based on an expanding debt Value balloon that moves Value created from nothing to players in the financial industry then bursts about every 10 years on the citizens. History shows us that after a century of this type of debt deception, the civilization is destroyed.

Central banks create currency when they buy "assets." For example, the U.S. Treasury creates bonds and the U.S. Central Bank (the Federal Reserve) creates money to buy the bonds. A U.S. Treasury bond is a debt issued by the United States that pays out an interest rate ("yield") based on the time period that it is held. The bond "asset" then sits on the balance sheet of the Fed and the dollars are then created for the U.S. Treasury. In another example, the Fed is now buying corporate bonds and creates the dollars to do so. The Fed also functions as an "overnight" lender, or lender of last resort, to big banks. Banks then create dollars through bank loans. The way this happens is that by law, banks can take your money on deposit then lend out 90 percent of it. This is officially called fractional reserve banking. The point of it is that the 90 percent of the deposit that is loaned out is then normally redeposited in the banking system, and then the banks can loan out from that another 90 percent, which is subsequently deposited into the banking system again and again.

The dollars created by banks from a $1,000 deposit will exceed $8,000 (detail in the Appendix). What this means to you is that the dollars that you deposit into your bank actually reduce the Value of all the dollars by the law of supply and demand. The work that you did to earn that deposit will lose a huge part of its Value, almost guaranteed.

The Greatest Deception is that saving your money in the bank in the form of the dollar and receiving less than 3 percent interest is smart and valuable and good. The Greatest Deception is that dollar creation does not hurt you and is great for the economy. Under the spell of the Greatest Deception, we have ignored the basic laws of supply and demand that dictate that the extra $8,000 dollars will make your $1,000 worthless because there are now more dollars chasing fewer goods. This makes prices go up over time. The deception is that the prices may rise for homes and cars and gas very quickly but for grocery items much more slowly and may not be noticed.

There's additional pressure. Banks not only lend out 90 percent of deposits but then spawn fractional contracts (derivatives) in the financial industry based on the paper that represent assets such as properties. These contracts can create dollars more than 30 times the original Value of the loan. Governments and banks then define the Value of real estate based on these contracts, and then tax and loan based on that real estate to perpetuity. Other financial products are then Valued relative to the Value of these contracts. Economies spawn derivative contracts on contracts, which then inflate the relative Value of not only the fiat dollars (currency issued without backing) created but also of every good and service on earth. Our use of this Value language is unsustainable.

In the year 2008, we saw the dollar balloon burst on the people in the United States and the world. Subprime mortgages were commonly named the culprit. But this crisis showed that the Emperor, the Dollar, had no clothes, as the homes had no dependable Dollar Value. It is important to stop here for a minute and reflect on how this dollar deception affected people and businesses. Some people who lost their businesses or careers are still deceived and look back at this time as their personal failure. This book is for you. Some executives may have heard of crypto technology but need a framework to make it useful. This book will uncover how these technologies will work for you. It is time to reset your business based on credible Value technologies and avoid the pitfalls of the past.

Enter Bitcoin and Blockchain

In 2008, a still unknown person named "Satoshi" unleashed a new technology named Bitcoin to solve this financial destruction. The technology works like cash money but is permanently coded to have a fixed supply. Its Value can be sent person-to-person without a bank involved. It is secured with a virtually unbreakable encryption.

Bitcoin is now entrenched in history and in the new economy of the world. The market players who buy it do not want to sell it or spend it because it is one of very few very liquid assets that continue to rise in Value compared to the dollars over time. Bitcoin has become a safe-haven asset for the world.

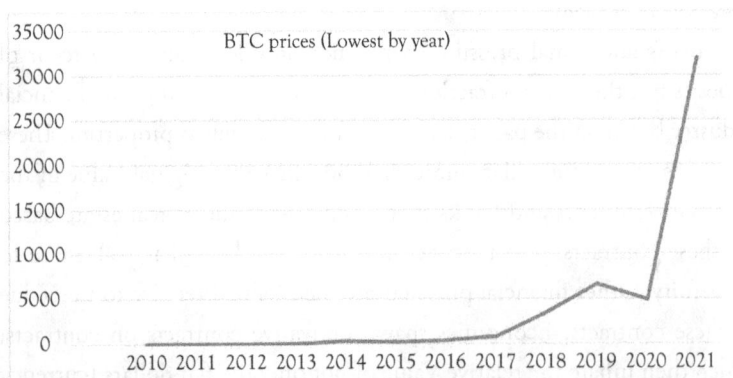

Figure 1.2 BTC price in USD over time

Source: Robertson 2021

Since 2010, a graph of Bitcoin price compared to the USD shows consistent higher lows, though some volatility is acknowledged.[2]

Bitcoin is the antithesis of the Greatest Deception because it has a fixed supply and an immutable accounting record of transactions locked using encryption that defines what transactions came before and after each (blockchain). This solution, including the ability to send payments without intermediaries, ignited a blockchain technology revolution that combined cryptographically secured transactions and records which then opened a new revolution in finance. The heart of the revolution in finance was that financial services could be automated and could function without banks using the security of the decentralized blockchain. The specific blockchain technology is named Ethereum.

The Ethereum revolution created technology that could tokenize, or synthetically represent, any item of Value. These digital representations of Value became part of a new financial system that can automate almost every financial function: loans, interest, derivatives, and markets and assets with technology sets called "smart contracts."

Ideal Value Language and Characteristics: Filling the Value Void

We can now create a new Value language that communicates Value more directly. First, we must address the question of how we can interpret Value so that business can cross language barriers, people groups, and different cultures. A bedrock Value system can be based on what is needed in common by everyone. These everyday items will serve as a new relative-Value base. With access to new information, it is possible to deliver a Value index that gives an effective way to communicate Value.

This book will propose how we can use comparable Values of a set of BHN as base for a Value language interpreter across the world; as a base for an "Information Currency." These would include items in the categories of food, shelter, basic clothing, paper products, and basic hygiene/medical items.

The items in these categories are distinctive not only as BHN but also because they are hard goods that will not spoil for at least a couple of years. The products also need to be easily transportable. The product set in its entirety should be easy to ship anywhere in the world on a container or in the bed of an airplane. This is important because these goods must represent an ability to pay someone who is distant, and not just transact in one area. The set of goods provides basic sustenance so that one could imagine its relief in a natural disaster to be enough for people to survive on. These goods become a standard (base) of Value.

With a core set of BHN "bank" of products, we will be able to compare which of these are available where, and at what Value around the world. Internet technology makes this information available at a near zero cost, free to most people. Given this critical information, we can seamlessly communicate the Value of a given set of goods related to other goods, all places, and comparable to all currencies.

The theory behind this method of Value language interpretation is based on the Law of One Price and related Purchasing Power Parity theory in Economics.[3] The Law of One Price basically says if there is trading in identical commodities that are exchanged in more than one market, in an efficient market there must be only one price for those identical commodities, regardless of where they are traded. So you can see that by establishing BHN items as a standard of Value, it's easier to encourage identical items that are traded in many different markets worldwide to have a comparable Value.

Technology can leverage this LOOP (Law of One Price) concept and algorithms to provide outcomes that ensure Purchasing Power Parity (where all buyers' purchasing power is equal, regardless of national currency) using a "basket" or "set" of these commodity products that may be traded between different economies. A transformation of Value language is possible based on the methods proposed in this book. If we own our Value language then we will own our work and our production.

The Players

The Current Role of Central Banks

Central banks create fiat currencies that are backed by the Nation States that issued them. (As previously noted, fiat currency is a national currency that is not pegged to the price of a commodity such as gold or silver. The Value of fiat money is largely based in the public's faith in the currency's issuer. Usually, the issuer is a country's government or central bank.)[4] The holders of the currency are dependent on a language of Value that can become irrelevant and imbalanced to the economies where it is used because there is no real or comparable

Value base. While using fiat currencies that are misinforming, one experiences distortions in purchasing power and it becomes very difficult to ascertain what causes it.

The way that Value language has been created, and the role that the central banks have played, could be called the Greatest Deception as was stated earlier. The central banks have been primarily responsible for creating our current dollar Value language because they hold the power to create money.

How is this so? How do the central banks create money?

A short explanation is that elite bankers who own the central banks are given this authority by the Nation. The Nation, through the central banks, forces its citizens to use the money that central banks create as a Value language for everything. This is called "legal tender," meaning that it is legal to use in the Nation for payments. The consequences are that a business is forced to accept this legal tender as payment and workers are forced to work for it.

The above is definitely a short explanation, because in practice there are some complications. For one thing, the central banks (such as the U.S. Federal Reserve) must abide by financial governance laws created by the Nation—and these laws are constantly changing. For instance, it used to be that the U.S. Federal Reserve (the Fed) could not directly buy stocks on the stock market using the money that the Fed printed. This rule changed in the year 2020. The Greatest Deception resulting from this law is that the stock market can look like it is doing very well while the economy is being simultaneously destroyed because the Fed pushes dollars into it to artificially prop it up.

Central banks move money into the financial system and money expands (more is "created") from fractional reserve rules (ones that allow banks to only hold a small portion of the money that they lend out) and from derivative financial engineering. Derivatives are a kind of financial instruments. They are basically a potentially risky casino of bets on bets—where the bet is on your house and the hedge (an investment done to offset possible losses) is also on your house—covered by insurers that cover only the "paper" representation of your home, not its real Value.

When the insurers have taken major losses in the past then governments bail them out (like the bailout of AIG in 2008).[5] Then the cycle of deception continues. In this cycle, the language of Value that we understood when we bought our homes was a deception and now suddenly, they are worth so much less. It would be most useful to move away from this kind of deception and vicious cycle and to make an equitable Value system that gives us a new Value language.

How Do Companies Now View Value

Companies primarily see and translate Value through dollar glasses. There is another way to see Value. If you are tired of seeing fixed assets depreciate, slow cash flow, and profits being absorbed by company growth then put on these new, vogue Value eyeglasses.

Company Value is customarily viewed by assets, cash flow, and profit by period. Our business culture focuses on these three parts as translated into a fiat dollar language.

Put on your new Value eyeglasses and let's start with assets. Consider how different and much broader your view of company Value would be if the assets were translated into who could use them. The dollar Value of a computer asset may be 2,000 in dollars. This Value depreciates normally based on standard accounting rules. What if you could rent out the space on your hard drive that you are not using today? There's a technology Value language for that. Since 2017, a company called IExec RLC (https://iex.ec) has worked on developing a blockchain design that allows businesses that need extra cloud storage or extra processing power to literally rent what is not used on another company's equipment.[6] The technology company designed the system in a unique way so that the borrowed computer space is separated between host computers for security and privacy. The only way that this tech could evolve was if the Value of the rented host computer could be capitalized in a method that the dollar cannot.

What about the forklift that is paid for? Can this asset be used to earn more income? There is a new Value language for that. Technology like that offered by companies such as Maker (https://makerdao.com/en), TinLake (https://tinlake.centrifuge.io), or Aave (https://aave.com) can turn your assets into a liquid Value based on an automated contract system on the blockchain.[7] The opportunity to tokenize assets with these technologies follows with an ability to use them as leverage for loans or to potentially exchange them as needed.

Here's yet another new idea to consider. What if cash flow could be translated into another asset that would be more profitable but just as liquid as cash? Cash dollars received by a business in a current time period is normally translated as Valuable because it is a liquid Value. What about the balance from cash flow in bank that accrued but is not used this week? There is a new Value translator for that. Those dollars can be exchanged into a currency whose Value increases. The technology to exchange dollars for many choices in cryptocurrency is simple to use. When you need the cash, then just transfer back to dollars what you need! Value in time can be capitalized more productively with a new Value language. (Disclaimer: the author is not a financial advisor, this is not financial advice, and the cryptocurrency markets can be volatile.)

See how bright the bottom line of the profit and loss statement would look if a company paid vendors and employees with its own products or services. Blockchain technology can capitalize or digitally represent (create a Value language for) a company's products and services. Using products such as Swarm Capital (https://swarm-capital.com) or Waves (https://waves.tech), or Open Sea (https://opensea.io) a company can more easily tokenize its products or services.[8] This is the opportunity brought into the light with Information Currency where Value is tokenized, thus capitalized as a new language using blockchain technology.

How Corporate Executives Manage Growth

Most executives drive growth for dollars

Executives drive company growth by focusing on cash margins denominated in dollars, assets Valued in dollars, loans in dollars, and bottom-line dollar profits. Executives accelerate sales for dollars, take growth speed limits in dollars, choose a dollar-flow highway and brake for dollar expenses, while often obsessing over the dollar-based accounting in the rearview mirror.

There is an alternative to driving for dollars. New technology makes new opportunities to drive for new capital in addition to dollars. The challenge to the executive is to utilize a new Value language. What this means is that the executive needs to think, communicate, and transact in new types of capital besides dollars.

A very straightforward explanation is made using an example with Bitcoin. When a businessperson first encounters this digital asset, he or she may be drawn in by the dollar profits possible by investing in the asset. Bitcoin purchases have been profitable in dollars for more than 90 percent of days in its history. Companies such as Tesla and Micro Strategy, and the Grayscale Bitcoin Trust are invested in Bitcoin. An executive who is practiced and fluent in driving to dollars may be excited to follow some financial and business leaders and purchase Bitcoin with a mindset of reaping the unusual dollar rewards.

But this executive, operating in a habit of a dollar-based language of Value, may be missing a real Value opportunity outside of that box. It may be that the executive should buy Bitcoin to secure the asset Value of the company and to enable the company to transact easily on the new financial highways that are being built.

On these highways, transactions are being permanently recorded on the blockchain. The executive can drive without the stress of constantly checking accounting in the rear-view mirror because the blockchain automatically keeps these records. On these highways, executives can take loans without banks. (The HOW-TO about this will follow in Chapter 4.) In these new financial vehicles, roads to new opportunities can be built on capital land that feels newly pioneered but has in fact been owned by the business for years. This all can happen when executives learn to speak in a capital language alternative to dollars.

The dollar is a vehicle, but it has rusted and broken down. Since 1972, it lost its new shine that it had during the time it was based on the gold standard. The vehicle's transmission is slipping, because it is impossible to depend on the Value of the dollar when the supply is increased by trillions. The speedometer is broken as velocity in the world economy slows. The headlight beams are weak and are failing to light up the way to the future because the dollar is not the future. You are. You will be sovereign.

We'll explain how you can do this in more detail a little later. But first, we will review the Value failure that almost every executive has experienced.

The Dead Market From Dollar
Value Information Failure

Proof of the failure of the dollar to report Value

We depend on dollar markets to give us real price discovery so that Value can be allocated. But property can be overValued in a market based on a credit bubble, like in 2008. Some dollar markets are dead. Evidence of a dead or nonproductive market is when an asset cannot be sold at any dollar price. A market that depends on dollars for transactions also depends on dollars for information about Value: What is available where, and at what Value.

The failure of the dollar to accurately report Value has been normalized—we blame the failure on something else. Here are some examples: if a product does not sell then we believe it was not advertised properly. If a product is overpriced in one area, then some business got lucky. If a person cannot find a job to match his or her skill, then that worker did not try hard enough. An unemployed worker is a nonproductive service in any society. We define goods that have not moved from a shelf for 12 months as dead stock. But if we focused on one city in the United States and detailed the dead stock in a spreadsheet, would it be worth nothing? The dollar has Valued these items at $0. The legal tender dollar has failed. There is proof of this if one can show that these items and services can capture Value after all.

In an eight-year study, specific research on the estimated Value of nonproductive stocks in building supply distributors in the United States was researched by Ruffin Trading Company, LLC (www.ruffintrading. com) in 2000 and showed that on average, 15 percent of inventories are nonproductive (meaning they have not turned over in 12 months). For a single distributor, this can be from $10,000 to $100,000 in inventories per location (Valued at average cost in USD). The company then proved that these inventories could regain Value using barter systems.

When an unemployed worker is offered his standard Value in pay in the form of his favorite restaurant coupon he will work. A building supply business will trade an entire wall of unsold hand tools for the same Value in software services. In fact, an entire industry exists based on dollar failure. This would be the barter (or trade) industry. What is the estimated

Value of the nonproductive stocks and services? The barter industry shows a total transaction Value of over 14 billion dollars (see the International Reciprocal Trade Association [IRTA] estimate at https://irta.com).

Why is the dollar system not working? One reason is that there are not enough dollars or enough credit in the system to operate economies at full capacity. Another reason is that the financial system has misdirected Values based on where central banks feed funding. But it is important to look at the Value all around us. Barter information proves that there are resources that we have right here in our world that are wasted and misdirected, including our own human capital. What is the opportunity cost of this dead stock? Ruffin Trading Company, LLC estimated in 2000 that it is equal to the Value of 10 percent–50 percent of the nonproductive stocks and services in the entire world minus the cost of implementing a technology and infrastructure, plus the exponential growth of this found capital in years to come. The time has come. The technology and infrastructure have arrived, and that will be instructed in this book.

Dollars hold us hostage to market failures evidenced by dead inventories and services without the Value and availability data that could be provided by an Information Currency secured by a base set of comparable, commoditized BHN items.

Value Issues: Store of Value

We depend on the dollar to store Value but this is not working

We have been told that dollars in a savings account are storing Value. But if the Central Bank in your country is printing currency, then your dollars in the bank are not storing Value and are, in fact, most likely losing Value.

Dollars do not have a Value language that we can trust to interpret the relative Value of things or to store Value in. We save and store dollars until we retire and then find that those dollars cannot buy half of what they used to. Between 2008 and 2011, the Value of our homes, property, and businesses crashed in dollar Value and these dollars are what we depended on to store the Value of our work. The year 2019 may have been the start of repeating this market tragedy. We need a new method to translate the Value of our work to the relative Value of property and other goods and services so that our store of Value is not erased.

The concept of Store of Value, though historically central to currency definition, is not needed for Information Currency. Instead, the store of Value can be directed to the item or service where the real Value is. Value is stored in the goods, services, and capital at market. Information Currency can go around alternative symbols of Value to reach and represent the market of goods and services directly. We may be able to avoid store of Value tragedies based on bad dollar information and currency market speculation if we can enable an Information Currency as a translator for the language of Value.

When there is excess Value, it can be assigned to Bitcoin and remain more secure over time, since—unlike dollars—the amount of Bitcoin that can exist is fixed—because the total number of Bitcoins will never exceed 21 million due to Bitcoin rules. And the excess Value will also be in a liquid form of Value that can be moved into other assets anywhere in the world as necessary.

More than 90 percent of the time that Bitcoin has been in existence it has increased in Value. Traditionally, we take excess Value in the form of dollars and leave them in a bank to lose Value until we use them. In this book, I will demonstrate how to take excess Value in dollars and move them to store Value in Bitcoin, then move them back to dollars only when there is a spending event. The technology to store Value in a form of money is easily available as an app right on our smart phones. These phone apps allow the user to buy major cryptocurrencies (including Bitcoin and Ethereum) with dollars and thus secure a "dollar Value" in them.

Dollars are still our primary Value language, and this traditional method of Value storage will be with us for a while. For this reason, we will need technologies to continuously translate dollar Value. Information Currency can be translated into various dollar languages by relying on a base index of the relative Value of what is real. Next, we'll look in more depth at what real Value is.

Market Value Is Real and Price Is Relative

Economists have always contested whether there is a real market Value (as conceptually distinct from "price") for items and services. Some of the legendary figures in economic thought favored an argument that

market Value is real and it is the price that is arbitrary. By understanding real Value, we can know how to capitalize on it in business.

Dollars, as in a form of U.S. currency, have been our primary source for information about Value and relative Value of every kind of good and service, including other dollar currencies. In using the dollar, we do not always get real capital information about Value. The dollar carries bad information when our basic source of stability, the dollar Value of our homes, suddenly falls or rises for irrational market reasons. The dollar carries bad information when a product has near-zero dollar Value because it has become nonproductive on business shelves, or when food in restaurants is not sold.

The dollar's misdirection about capital Value is proven by the $14 billion barter industry, as it capitalizes lost Value every day from products and services that had become dead stock—but which are quickly consumed on trade at full retail Value. Take, for example, the hotel with extra rooms, the accountant with extra time, the restaurant with extra food that will spoil, or the distributor with excess, dead, or nonproductive stock. The barter industry provides information in an organized manner about these excesses, and they are consumed at full Value by those who also are willing to provide the information about excess.

Since its beginning, the Internet has made more Value and availability information accessible to the market than ever before in history. This information about capital has made massive changes to industry structure. It has brought into business those who contribute to market information efficiently and put out of business those who do not. These changes were necessary for businesses to move into the age of information. As the Internet has become the technical base for moving information about Value and availability, concepts of currency structure and Value language about capital now have new frontiers.

Given this new window of Big Data and access to this capital Value information all over the world, we no longer need an intermediary like the dollar between transactions, and we do not need a central bank to issue such. In fact, we will discover and identify Value directly in the capital products and capital services themselves and simply move their entity assignments around in the market. Information about the items themselves makes them capitalized and then this information becomes the currency.

Economists have always contested whether there is a real market Value (as conceptually distinct from "price") for items and services. Some of the legendary figures in economic thought including Adam Smith, considered labor as a base of Value and others who related commodity capital and land as a base of Value, favored an argument that market Value is real and it is the price that is arbitrary. Capital Value is important because by understanding real Value we can know how to capitalize on it. Information is no longer scarce. We can be sure that our idea and language of Value will begin to translate more clearly when we have real information about what is available, where it is, and at what relative Value—and then capitalize on it.

The Dollar Is Information About its Value

We depend on the Value language of the dollar to properly Value items in our world but there are other Value languages that show us more relevant truth about what things are worth.

The dollar, such as other fiat currencies, shows us information about its Value. We do not think of the dollar as a Value that can change relative to what it can buy. It is more common to think of what the dollar can buy as changing. The dollar today can functionally give you the Value to buy a cup of coffee selling for $1. The dollar tomorrow, maybe, might not give you enough Value to buy that SAME cup of coffee. If tomorrow it costs $1.10, it would be normal to blame the seller who raised the price from yesterday and believe that he just wants more dollars for his coffee. But from the perspective of a trader (someone who is familiar with making transactions that do not use currency), it may be that the dollar has less Value, because now it takes more of them to satisfy the owner of the coffee.

But this language misinforms. For instance, it allows people to think that land does not have an intrinsic, stable Value. In dollar language, the dollar is stable, and the land has shifting Value. In your dollar Value language, your dollar Value is stable but eggs at the grocery store from the same farm in the same city randomly have less Value today relative to dollars (cost more) yesterday. Dollar Value information misinforms the market.

So how then is the dollar information? Remembering our example of trading eggs for coffee discussed earlier, since we would have to pay one more egg to get our coffee, we now know that eggs now are worth less relative to the Value of coffee. If eggs were used to pay for everything then we'd know a whole lot about the Value of eggs relative to every other kind of good and service. All that the eggs end up doing is providing information about Value. If we logged the relative Value of eggs compared to other goods, we would then know how to derive additional product Value information. For instance, if we also traded eggs for pigs, then we might know more about the Value of pigs compared to coffee. In these trade events the eggs become an alternative language for Value information.

The dollar is not able to consistently store or interpret Value information. This means that if you speak the dollar Value language, you may not see things of Value. But dollar Value language can be interpreted. New tools can show information about relative Value. With the tools discussed in this book it may soon feel like you can put on special night-vision goggles to be able to see new opportunities, new Value, new finance, and new chances for security and growth.

Redefining Currency With Pure Information

Examples and discussion of how direct trade is a method of using Information as currency

The dollar is a symbol of Value, and that language symbol carries an identity with a certain amount of goods and services. This is evident when you visit another country because when you go to purchase an everyday item it is difficult to guess how much of that foreign currency language to use. If items were priced in your type of dollars, then the language of Value would feel fluent as related to a Value for familiar goods. The tools that are primarily used for currency exchange, or translation, are the foreign exchange (FOREX www.forex.com) and "Xe" (www.xe.com) markets. The FOREX is still used as our main interpreter of dollar languages. These markets are for currency speculation and the traders focus on profit. For this reason, the FOREX is not always accurate as a dollar Value language translator.

Direct information can be a better translator for Value exchange. As we have mentioned, pure information is currency when it can inform what is available, where it is, and at what relative Value. This direct information makes the medium of exchange unnecessary. An exchange of Value using pure information would be direct barter, or corporate trade. Real examples include: British tennis shoes traded for Russian vodka, Jamaican coffee traded for Japanese Toyota cars, and French ceramic tiles traded for a JCB forklift. In these real-life cases, the currency and the Value translation was pure information. That is information currency.

Another example of pure information Value language for exchange would be a trade through a retail barter exchange. The retail barter exchange accounts for the balances between small business members. Members see lists of other members and their goods offered for trade. The retail barter exchange operates as a third-party record keeper, but the members go on to purchase what they need based on the information of items and services available. In the retail barter environment, pure information is the language of exchange. Information is the currency in retail barter exchange.

New technology structures of tokenization and automated exchanges are similar to barter functions which add asset tracking built to manage direct information for use as a Value language. These basic data structures move asset information from the real world into a synthetic, digital world. The synthetic representation of real-world data is then secured and managed on a blockchain where the data and transactions are then immutable (unchangeable). This means that the vodka that is manufactured in the real world also has a digital, synthetic representation. So do the Reebok tennis shoes. The physical items exist as assigned to the manufacturer. The process to make this real involves moving the material world data to the synthetic world, and it involves securing the item information in a way that is as critical as it is to build a fence around the manufacturer's property to secure their product in the real world.

The token security is important because these synthetic information representations are now real Value. An identity for the vodka is made on the blockchain and every transaction, including the one for Reebok shoes, is permanently recorded. There are no dollars required in the transaction. This is information currency in the making.

The job of validating real asset information to the blockchain can be performed by what is called an *oracle*:

> An oracle is a way for a blockchain or smart contract to interact with external data. With blockchains being deterministic one-way streets, an oracle is the path between off-chain and on-chain events. Inbound oracles bring off-chain or real-world data to the blockchain, whereas their outbound cousins do the opposite: they inform an entity outside the blockchain of an event that occurred on it.[9]

An oracle is technology that validates real-world data to the synthetic and secure world on the blockchain. Oracles are not the currency, but in many ways operate as one of the structures that facilitate and validate the reality of—Information Currency.

Information About Real Value

In order to measure real Value, we need a consistent unit of measure and dollar Value language is not providing this.

The history of currency operating as a unit of measure can be easily understood by looking at coins where literally the measure (weight) of the metal (gold or silver, for instance) was the Value of the coin. The metal coin was a fitting standard. Central bank currencies such as the USD are thought to function like a unit of measure (one dollar), but today it is only fiat money (not commodity backed). In our culture for the past five decades, the Value of the dollar in everyday life is a language that may feel like a true measure of Value. A dollar can buy standard things that we all know, like a Hershey bar, a bag of chips, a gallon of gas, and a dozen eggs. In this way, it is a measure of Value. We may forget that 10 years ago that same dollar would buy two Hershey bars, two bags of chips, two gallons of gas, a whole gallon of milk, and two dozen eggs.

Over time, it is easy to prove that this dollar unit of measure is not a standard. Consider as a comparison how a foot ruler is a unit of measure consisting of 12 inches. Has a ruler changed in the last 10 years? No. How would a culture respond to a changing size of an inch or a meter? Wouldn't we have chaos? We are deceived into thinking that a dollar is a standard unit of measure and is something that we can rely on to under-stand Value. This is not the case. Ideally, a standard should be unchanging, as in the analogy of the 12 in. ruler. A standard of Value should be relevant to what every human and every society needs. The standard can be an item, such as a bottle of water or a bag of rice and the item, or a group of items, can be used to determine the unit. The bottle of water, then, becomes the unit of measure. The bag of rice or pound of coffee is the unit standard. A set of basic goods can be the new unit standard of measure and everything else is a relative Value to that standard. The dollar language would be reversed. Instead of how many dollars does the can of tuna cost it would be how many cans of tuna does the dollar cost. In this standard, the dollars are costed in bottles of water. The dollars are costed in bags of rice. This ideal standard of measure and standard of Value is completely possible to manage with existing technology.

The challenge to implement this change is not the technology any-more. The first challenge is about Value language. In the beginning, we will need to constantly use a tool to convert from dollar language to this new standard. The first step is to provide the relative Value information about the new standard. For the new standard, we will need to know how many dollars that bag of rice can buy in my town compared to another. Then how many dollars that bag of rice can buy in another state. Then how many Euros the bag of rice can buy, and so on throughout the world. This first step is important to take into account for an entire set of BHNs, as each is like a new word in a new language.

The second challenge is to scale to an entire set of BHN products. We will learn how many dollars the entire set of BHN products can buy. This information as a ratio by nation can be a new standard of Value. Every other product and service can be Valued from this basis. This ratio will show the Greatest Deception and can free us from its control.

How to Compare Information Currency to Central Bank Currency

A central bank typically issues new currency directly into the financial system by purchasing financial assets. This creates a situation where this new money may not reach the citizens who work to produce products and provide services.

When new fiat dollars are created by Central Banks then there is more money chasing the same amount of goods and services. This makes goods and services more expensive over time, so the dollars have less purchasing power. As a result, the workers get depreciating (less and less) Value from their work.

Economist Richard Cantillon warned about the result of central banks funneling dollars to a specific sector of the economy and how concentrated wealth in that sector would result. The problem with extreme concentrated wealth in a society is that this can reduce the velocity of money (how often money changes hands), and as a result, the viability of an economy. We were warned of the Cantillon effect more than two hundred years ago.[10]

Alexander Hamilton, an economist and one of the Founding Fathers of the United States, also had a grip on the danger of a central bank with the power to print paper money.

Hamilton famously wrote that "the proper funding of the present debt will render it a national blessing." But he less famously added that "the creation of debt should always be accompanied with the means of extinguishment [of that debt]."

"Steer clear of paper money," Hamilton urged the central bank that he had not yet instituted. No wise government would trust itself with "so seducing and dangerous an expedient."

"In times of tranquility," Hamilton goes on, "it might have no ill consequence, it might even perhaps be managed in a way to be productive of good; but in great and trying emergencies, there is almost a moral certainty of its becoming mischievous. The stamping of paper is an operation so much easier than the laying of taxes, that a government, in the practice of paper emissions, would rarely fail in any such emergency to indulge itself too far, in the employment of that resource, to avoid as much as possible one less auspicious to present popularity. If it should not even be carried so far as to be rendered an absolute bubble, it would at least be likely to be extended to a degree, which would occasion an inflated and artificial state of things incompatible with the regular and prosperous course of the political economy."[11]

Without clear rules related to a solid proof of backing to a currency, a central bank with the power to issue legal tender currency is essentially a blank check with the name of the citizens of this country and their children and children's children as payee.

There is not freedom to make real Value when citizens must speak dollar Value language. Central banks make us enslaved to their language and distribution of Value. When there is a quantitative easing event (when central banks buy financial assets to create dollars), the dollars made become Value assigned and spoken over the sector or business to whom it is sent. Citizens must then work for those sectors of society. This is not freedom or a free society.

Older than central bank currencies are alternative currency models built on trade. At a time where the world economy is so fragile, this ideation of freedom of Value is exactly what we need now. This idea of Information Currency will evolve and introduce a new type of free society as an alternative to being gamed by our current monetary system.

Barter as Information Currency

Barter is a language that tells what is available where and at what relative Value to another good or service.

Barter is a form of Information Currency as it reports what is available where and at what relative Value. As an example, we can look at stories of how small towns in the United States old West traded in bygone days. In the general store, customers who wanted to buy wheat might bring in some of their crafted knives. Or the doctor might offer his services to a family in town to trade for eggs every week. In small communities, everyone knew what goods and services were available and their relative Value without even a currency. The family that raised the chickens paid for almost everything with eggs. The knife-maker did the same. The doctor traded services for almost everything and that relative Value was just known. Yes, there was gold. There were also dollars "backed" or secured with gold as each dollar was redeemable for a specific amount of gold or silver.

Our new technology has brought us to a point where we have the capability to go back and exchange goods and services like that small town out West. The reason it is worth using this technology is because we, the people, need to own our production. When we use central bank-issued currency, it is like forcing everyone in that Western town to pay for everything in eggs. When this happens, the egg supplier takes power, and every transaction is relevant to the egg supplier. If one of the chickens goes down, then there are fewer eggs and this translates into a small town market where the people that had the eggs control the market. The inequities continue and the market in that town becomes imbalanced. In another scenario, if everyone in the town can only pay in gold the market is limited by how much gold is available and how the gold supplier decides to trade. The gold supplier might trade with a few people in town and then hoard the gold. This is what happens with dollars as well.

The freedom in the barter town is that instead of one supplier taking power where every other good and service is defined in the Value language of that supply item, every good and service (and any kind of money) could be used as currency. This really can happen, and a great example is in a small town with good communication. The way this works is that everyone in town knows about almost every trade and transaction so from these patterns a language of relative Value is developed.

If, for instance, the local restaurant buys eggs from the farm every Monday then the egg Value relative to other items in town may be higher on Monday. The doctor might be showered with all kinds of production from town during flu season. If the doctor in town had a big family that needed to have eggs on Monday, he could go up to the chicken farm and make a deal where he would get some eggs on Monday in exchange for his doctor services for the farm family. That family then secures the doctor's visits during flu season. This barter deal where nontransacted Value is secured and assigned is the critical store of Value element in the definition of money.

The deal between the doctor and the farm as the store of Value might work on their promise in a small town. In a bigger town, the deal might need to be secured with tickets. For example, the doctor might give three tickets for doctor services worth three visits and the farm would give the doctor tickets for five dozen eggs. When the doctor picks up two dozen eggs, those two tickets are given back to the farm.

In the world today, we function with about one generic "ticket" (dollar) type per country, but the USD tickets are redeemable for almost any other country's dollar tickets. The national dollar tickets are not printed to match the amount of goods and services that a nation provides, like the tickets for the eggs and the doctor services in the small town. This situation is not economically sustainable.

The new technologies for tickets are called tokens. Token technology is just a representation of a service or an asset and sometimes for an idea. But token technology is unique because tokens are made from automated contracts called "smart" contracts. The contract is usually initiated by its owner. So, the egg farm can decide that it will produce 100 dozen eggs and can make a contract for 100 egg tokens. The egg tokens are often assigned in the beginning to the entity that initiated the contract. The technology secures the tokens with better-than-military-grade encryption. In this way, the token ticket can assume real Value which means that if the doctor receives egg tokens, he can be sure he holds the Value of eggs. The technology automatically records every transaction of the token with every entity, whether it is a doctor or the farm. The transaction records are called a ledger, in the same way that we use the word in accounting. As we have mentioned previously in the definition of blockchain, the ledger technology is called a blockchain because it secures in transaction order by "blocks" or groups of orders. The magic of blockchain is that the blocks, or groups of transactions, are encrypted just like the tokens, so that no one can ever change the record of what happened.

Imagine in the Western town that the chicken farm could make egg tokens and the knife maker could make knife tokens and the doctor could make tokens representing his services. The Ethereum cryptocurrency was the first platform to easily enable this technology. It gives us the ability to use smart contracts to create secure tokens that are digital representations of assets and services.

Since these tokens have real Value, the chicken farm needs a vault to hold them! The knife maker and the doctor need a vault too. To make it easy, the technology includes entity assignments that are called wallets and can be named like their owners. So the tokens can be assigned to the wallet entity called chickenfarm.crypto or sent to westerndoctor.crypto. Technically the token Value assignment is to a pair of a series of numbers and letters where one of the pair is public and one is the encrypted private one. The tokens and the wallets are part of the necessary store of Value for Information Currency.

Ethereum automated ("smart") contracts can create tokens that are fungible (where the tokens are interchangeable) because they basically represent the same asset in the same measure. A smart contract that minted egg tokens would be like this. Dollars work like this too. But there are also Ethereum-based tokens that are designed to represent assets that are unique, like a token representing a doctor's specific surgery, or a work of art, or a house. Unique tokens are called nonfungible tokens—they are a special type of cryptographic token that represents something unique. Later in the book in Chapter 9 are hands-on instructions to get a real feel for wallets and tokens.

When tokens are created on the Ethereum blockchain, they are encrypted into a defined identity and are ready for trading. Every transaction is recorded. The token functions as a store of Value and as a unit of measure. The token is a defined and specific type of unit of measure plus its every move is automatically and permanently stored. Ethereum makes blocks, or groups of transactions that are securely processed and then permanently encrypted in order. This blockchain technology has significance because the function of the token exchange, and the permanent record of the exchange, allows the blockchain to become the medium of exchange. The tokens are transacted on the blockchain between entities and these transactions are permanently recorded as a chain of transaction blocks.

To summarize, we can represent our goods and services with secure, synthetic, and digital representations. The goods and services can be assigned to virtual entities in secure wallets. We can have permanent and secure accounting of transactions anywhere in the world. The Information Currency technology that works today essentially enables the world to barter just like that old Western town. The technology functions according to all three definitions of currency: Unit of Measure, Store of Value, and Medium of Exchange. This technology gives people the ability to directly own their work and their production. In this way, Information Currency allows us to speak and hear our own Value language.

We all need to speak and hear our own Value language, but we will also need technology to help us translate into other languages as well. The whole world of virtual barter is a much more complex environment than in the Western town. Soon the world will frantically tokenize everything, and with the entire world able to shout out their Value in tokens, how will we communicate with all that Value noise? We can execute a translation plan for this great paradigm shift because we can't live for long in Babel land.

Paradigm Changes for Value Language

The first paradigm shift for the language of Value was the discovery of free Value information.

The Internet made information about Valuation free and accessible to anyone. It is now normal to think of something that you want to buy and then look it up on online to get an idea of that item's Value. This information is a critical beginning piece to Information Currency. Known Values drive markets. Markets soon become slaves to expectations, and consumers make choices based on Values that they demand. The more information about Value and availability of items, the more consumers will shift and pressure markets to meet a rational equilibrium.

Free information about what is available where and at what Value was the first paradigm shift in our language of Value. The world experienced a similar challenge during the Internet revolution. Suddenly the world had an overload of information about what was available where and at what Value. Initially Value data was siloed in websites that belonged to companies. Then companies such as eBay, Google, and others made it easy to look up an item or service and reference its Value information from different silos.

When business was able to invoice on the Internet and deliver real products and services from an online order, we entered the *second* paradigm shift in our language of Value. We could move Value without being in-person and without even speaking. The information alone about what products were where at what Value was leveraged by companies such as Amazon and Alibaba and made the new Value information from the former paradigm shift real. During this paradigm shift, Amazon built its base. By gaming Value information about each item, Amazon in particular was able to profit by speaking a new relative Value language. The company understood that by comparing Value information by item (the "what") and by coordinating and making deals for the distribution of the "where and at what Value" they would survive and thrive during the paradigm shift of the Internet revolution. Many of the siloed suppliers who did not address the new open information succumbed to Amazon.

The collapse of dollar Values in 2008 ignited Satoshi, the anonymous designer of Bitcoin, to create a totally new language of Value. With this technology, we entered another, *third* paradigm shift with a concept that a tokenized and secure representation of Value, freely transferable, with fixed quantity parameters could provide a trustable store of Value. Though originally intended to be used fluently as currency, continued to increase in Value compared to dollars over time and became a kind of "gold language" to most holders. Seven years later Ethereum, designed by Vitalik Buterin, began the token Value road. Soon after, technologies that supported this Value road sought funding for their projects through initial coin offerings and the funding to build this vast new Value interstate began.

The paradigm shift number *four* was the fascinating realization that tokens representing Value could be used to realize and gain Value in time. The DeFi technologies started around 2017 but got solid footing in 2020. What this shift did was prove how the technology of blockchain, encryption, and tokenization could secure Value over time. Rising out of memories about the deep dark hole of the Great Recession in 2008, from the trauma of lost homes, lost businesses, lost jobs, and lost Value period, the DeFi movement—involving financial services with no central authority—inspired the markets with real Value traction. It is a Value language leap to conceive that anything can be tokenized and that every token has an opportunity to realize its leverage. To break that down, in this new Value language, any tokenized asset is functionally able to store Value, be leveraged for loans, or to earn interest. Not just the dollar.

The *fifth* shift in our language of Value to come will be a collapse of dependence on dollar languages to speak Value about products and services. The Greatest Deception of dollars diluted by currency price inflation and directed to specific sectors in the economy will be revealed. Going forward, the dollar languages can be measured by information about the relative Values of commodities. Commodities are similar items with known Values around the world. Societies will refuse to speak dollars without translating their Value into a relative Value to standard, needed items. In the *fifth* paradigm shift, the language of Value will gain traction by indexing the Values of commodities. This set of commonly needed items will likely become the standard translator of relative Value around the world.

In the *sixth* Value paradigm to come every tokenized item and service in the world will be like a word in the new Value language. It will be free of governments, independent of banks, transferable, assignable, fit to be leveraged or invested at will, and secure from deception. This is the new paradigm of liberty; to speak a Value language over which we are sovereign.

To recap, the *first* paradigm shift for the language of Value was the discovery of free Value information. The *second* paradigm shift allowed Amazon and Alibaba business models to actualize the Value information. The *third* paradigm birthed Bitcoin and Value tokenization. The *fourth* Value paradigm has tokenized Value in time for financial structure.

The *fifth* paradigm will use relative Value standards as tools for translating and exchanging Value. The *sixth* paradigm will virtually and completely ideate Value Language by tokenizing what is available, where, and at what relative Value.

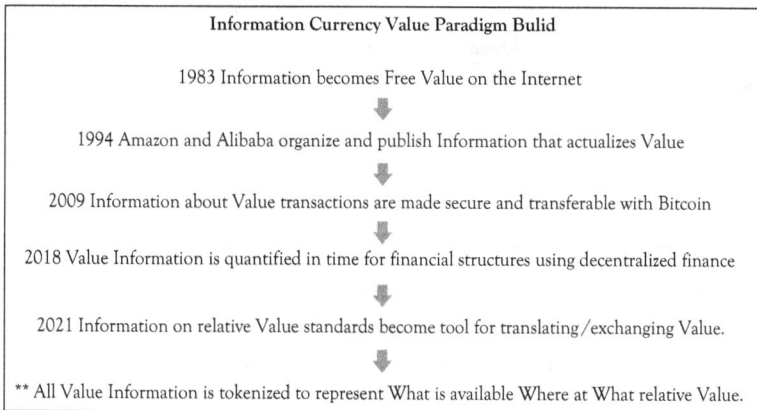

Information Currency Value Paradigm Bulid

1983 Information becomes Free Value on the Internet

⬇

1994 Amazon and Alibaba organize and publish Information that actualizes Value

⬇

2009 Information about Value transactions are made secure and transferable with Bitcoin

⬇

2018 Value Information is quantified in time for financial structures using decentralized finance

⬇

2021 Information on relative Value standards become tool for translating/exchanging Value.

⬇

** All Value Information is tokenized to represent What is available Where at What relative Value.

Figure 1.3 Building an information currency paradigm

Source: Robertson 2021

Translating Value Language

We need a common Value language that every human can use to compare Value of any product or service in the world.

This consideration to begin with invokes just pure Value language awe. Most every human on earth can name almost every item around them this minute and assign a number, a Value in their dollar Value language. To perform this act in another kind of dollar language most every human would need a conversion tool.

We are so binary in our thinking, and this is a problem. The conventional Value language translating tool is the FOREX, which considers currency conversion (a ratio of an amount of one currency to another) in binary pairs; dollars to euros, dollars to pesos, euros to pesos, and the other way around, and so forth. Why this is a problem is it prevents the world from seeing a more fluid, whole Value picture.

To explain this using a barter example, a common misconception about barter is that it is only a one-to-one trade ... binary, of course. Barter in professional methods often requires at least three, more often five, and most of the time even more transactions to get from A to B. Value and opportunity are diluted in a binary Value world. For example, a dentist wants to eat dinner at a Mexican restaurant. The dentist offers the Mexicans his services (the dentist-Mexican restaurant pair). The Mexicans are not interested in exchanging their food for getting their cavities filled. The dentist asks what the restaurant needs. They need new menus from a printer. So, the dentist finds a printer who needs his or her teeth fixed, and the printer gives menus to the Mexicans and the dentist finally gets his Mexican dinner. In conclusion, if paired, the Mexican-Dentist pair equals zero. But the Mexican-Dentist-Printer has Value. In our future, Value languages will look a lot more like this than like FOREX. The barter industry has developed in this way.

From the viewpoint of most cryptocurrency advocates, the Value problem is all about central banks printing dollars and that the Value solution is the quantified, published, and limited supply of each cryptocurrency.[12]

So, if a currency has a finite quantity, such as Bitcoin, or a relatively finite supply, like gold, then the currency will have a great Value language. But some of this focus on scarcity is a traumatic reaction to the continuous currency creation by the U. S. Federal Reserve (the *Greatest Deception*) and other countries, from the early 1970s up until its explosion starting in 2019.

We know that too much currency printing creates a currency dilution that leads to disaster. The point to see is that, though defining the scarcity of a currency will solve one Value problem there are more Value challenges to consider. For example, if today, we had to buy a dozen eggs with Bitcoin, a currency with a defined supply, would we have any idea how many *sats* that would cost? (*Sats* are a smaller denomination of Bitcoin). Can we depend on the cryptocurrency exchanges to translate Value? Cryptocurrency and dollar exchanges are driven by profit-driven traders who focus on pairs. The crypto and dollar exchange information may assist us at checkout, but not as much with our Value language translation (as in how many *sats* are a dozen eggs worth?). Living in a multi-currency world, we will need a guide to help us decide if the eggs—and every other item—are a fair deal in the currency their price is quoted in.

Value language should be discovered in markets. But relative Values cannot be discovered very well in a binary Value language. If we continue to try to speak Value language in binary dollars-to-products and dollars-to-services and dollars-to-dollars, then our economies will miss market opportunities and real price discovery will fail.

It is a myth that markets in their current form will make dollar currencies work efficiently and transparently. The first reason for market inefficiency is information asymmetries (Investopedia defines market inefficiency in this way). Markets have always had scarce information about what is available, where, and at what Value. Without the aid of new Value technology, price discovery using dollars will continue to just guess at markets.

What has already been achieved with the tokenization of products and services will enhance our Value language. The technology that enables a medium and record of exchange with blockchain will also increase our ability to speak and translate Value languages. What we have yet to achieve is to enable a Value base where all humans can see the market. We need a common thread to connect us all to markets where information is currency, and currency is information in a language that we all can understand.

The quest for a universal Value base is a deep, gaping black hole in our market mentality. The vacancy, emptiness, and depth of this hole in our markets is so severe that in the moments that we see the edge of it, the moment that we have a flash of realization of it, and the second that we look into the obvious we turn away and revert to our stone-age speak. But we need to go back and look into that hole.

More than 20 years ago at the IRTA meeting, the members agreed that the number one challenge in the barter industry was the lack of a standard for Value. These brave members were virtually standing around and looking down into the black hole. Back then it was progressive just to name the challenge. But now, with the technology we can claim and have made real today, we need to send all of our best men and women in tech over to that jobsite.

At this Value black hole jobsite, we see dollars as an apparition, a specter, and a mirage as a Value base. Some folks are saying again, "believe in gold." But gold was just the asphalt for the road to the place we are in now, still looking into that black hole. Then Bitcoin built a virtual skyway bridge over the hole, and we still only did not look down. Now Ethereum has brought in cranes (technology to transact and tokenize Value) and Polka-Dot (a crypto project designed to integrate different blockchains) new lanes (meaning, blockchain interoperability so that tokens and information can be exchanged seamlessly across blockchains). And with all of this build-out we are ready with technology, and we have the privilege *for the first time in history* to ask the question, *What do we want to be the base of Value for all of us in the world?*

The reality at our doorstep is that there are 180 central bank style dollar (fiat) currencies used by 195 countries in the world. There are over 2,000 cryptocurrencies available to the world to transact in. In addition, there are tokenized representations of companies, contracts, futures, services, and physical assets. In this new reality, we will need new tools to transition to think of and to translate Value. In this transition, we will need a guide for comparison. We will need a common language that every human can compare to any product or service in the world.

Until we answer these questions, our best technology and our best men and women in tech will be unable to circumvent the debasement of Value of nature, of labor, and of humanity. These misplaced Value systems have led to dysfunctional, zero-sum, and gamed markets, where nothing is believed to be of real Value to society but the winner.

CHAPTER 2

Devising a New Value Language

Filling the Value Void by Making a Bedrock Value Decision

Why do we need to define bedrock common Value? Because a world where there is a digital representation of virtually everything physical and everything of Value is approaching us at light speed.

Tokenization technology is advancing so quickly that it may arrive before we have a chance to understand why. This is why; with every digital thing there will soon be an opportunity to make new Value and make new markets, and these markets will experience a trading velocity unlike any we have ever seen. With this transition, it is even possible that we may experience near zero-Value dollars and infinite digital asset representations simultaneously. The old markets will go toward zero and the new digital representations will capture the Value. This future is unfolding as well-respected corporate executives like Michael Saylor (founder of MicroStrategy), Elon Musk (CEO of SpaceX and Tesla, Inc.), Raoul Pal (CEO of Real Vision Group and Global Macro Investor), Jack Dorsey (CEO of Twitter), and Chamath Palihapitiya (CEO of Social Capital) lead the way by making major purchases of digital assets to show their nod toward this future.

The Internet revolution will be diminutive compared to the sea-change and velocity of markets transformed when digital representations are used for trade. We will look back on the concept of a dollar as an archaic Value language where we had to use a medium of exchange and binary methods to accomplish a transaction. Information about relative Values will become the currency language, as currency will be information about digital representation of things. We will need new tools, new ratios, and new relative Value systems to guide us. We will need to learn a new Value language.

A way to think about it is to imagine that society will revert to a system of barter, as in goods for goods, goods for service. This transaction environment will be possible because our technology will enable every good and service to be represented in digital form. At this point, we will feel almost lost like the folks at the Tower of Babel. We will need a guide (a translator) for relative Value.

When we enter this era, that may be unimaginable to some, we will naturally gravitate to comparing Value by using familiar items to understand relative Value. Of course, what is familiar is our old concept of our dollars. But as the transactions go faster and become more significant, we will need a Value guide; a Value translator to gauge relative Value of dollar currencies. This can work like an exchange rate but it will not be binary. Current technologies like Loopring (https://loopring.io) bring multiple digital asset transactions together in this way. The Loopring technology makes speedy, low-cost transactions by running sets of transactions on a layer on top of Ethereum, which rolls up sets of transactions (batches) at a time. Multiple digital assets are "pooled" to share constantly fluctuating relative Values with technologies like Balancer (https://balancer.finance) and Curve (https://curve.fi).

Technologies such as Yearn (https://yearn.finance) search through pools of relative Values of tokens to find the best relative asset yield.[1,2]

In a similar way, information about commodities (similar items with a generally known Value) can be used to create information organization where the guide or relative Value index is automated. Given a big enough sample set of items that most people use in common it is possible to generate statistics that automate comparable Value standards. Technologies such as Synthetics (https://synthetix.io) can be used to digitally represent commodities and track Values. We will need increasingly more of them to guide us through transactions.

This technology used now is based on decentralized networks. The decentralized networks are different computers that host and verify the same blockchain. These networks validate information about digital asset transactions on multiple nodes (a node is a computer operating as part of the network) from multiple sources. Oracle technologies such as

Chainlink, Band, DOS (Decentralized Oracle Service), and API3 can send real-world price data to the blockchain to inform these transactions.[3]

To focus on the most relevant Value guide, it is important to look at what items can be standard globally. An additional consideration is if there is a moral cause to consider basing the Value system on items that humans need in common. Is it of moral Value to be sure to include commodities such as soap, rice, and bottled water? We have never been faced with such a clear and important opportunity to decide what items represent a common bedrock of Value in the world.

What has been the bedrock common Value language of our world for the last 50 years? Is real Value oil or gold or militias or natural resources? We need to build our Value bedrock before the critical demands of business for all of humanity are sidelined. We need to enable this bedrock before a new *Great Deception* echoes like another ghost of Value rising from that black hole into a world that just could not make that decision.

The Case for a Basic Human Needs Value Base

The question is, *what do we want the base of Value for all of us in the world to be?*

The answer to this "black hole of Value" question is to use the relative Values of basic human needs (BHN). BHN, essential items that every human from every economic and ethnic background needs to survive, are the five categories of food, building materials, clothes, paper products, and hygiene/medical supplies. These items represent the bedrock of common Value. Imagine about 50 items in the five distinct categories that would be sent for human survival in the event of a disaster. These products in barter are the most liquid products in the world. This means that they are easily saleable or transferable because almost every human being uses them.

This idea is derived from years of evidence in the barter industry where all trades can be paid in basic needed hard good items. In barter practice, when a business brings an item to the barter market to trade it is often met with a customer who has no use for that item or service. In the example of the dentist, even though many people can use this service, it is not always needed in time. In the earlier example of the printer, the services are useful but not always needed every day by every customer. In the earlier example of Mexican food, some people may not have a taste for this every day or maybe not at all. Each one of these companies and every person in these companies would take payment in BHN items. In the case that the dentist and the restaurant and the printer had enough BHN then they could easily transfer this need to their families, employees, or for payment to their suppliers. Even if these coffers were full, the BHN items could be stored for use later.

For a different perspective, if there was a store that exclusively stocked BHN items, then the store could issue tickets to trade with any person or entity. This liquidity, transferability, usability, ability to store, and universal need fills the deep Value void as bedrock of Value for the world. The set of items can be represented with existing technology and used for Value comparisons, and these relative Values would be derived from the Value bedrock. In this example, information about these relative Values is currency, and currency is information about relative Values used to transact as a currency.

If businesses do not step up to the plate and participate in building a new Value bedrock then we will give up our own Value, the Value of our work, the Value of our heritage, and the Value of our nations to the highest bidder, who will again be the only winner. Barter has never been a zero-sum game and our technology can resurrect the oldest method of transacting that mankind has known into a new tech world where we win together.

Choosing a New Currency Base

The Item Banc open protocol is proposed in this book for technology to enable this Value base.

Capitalizing Commodities to Translate Value

A commodity is a similar product or service with a known Value around the world. We can commoditize the set of BHN items for the purpose of creating a base of Value. With a base set, or basket of products, we can compare Values of other items in the market by

comparing the ratio of the basket Value to similar baskets around the world. This contributes to an overall understanding of relative Value of currencies. In Economics, a similar exercise is referred to as Purchasing Power Parity—which you may remember from an earlier mention of the term.

We can use information systems to compare real-time Values of similar items around the world to commoditize BHN products. Normally a commodity may have a qualitative difference and it does not matter what brand it is. Commodities are not exactly the same. Coffee, for example, is a commodity and highly differentiated. A commodity Value does not mean that the commodity will have the exact same selling price for each transaction. This is important to establish because we need to make clear that we need to make BHN into commodities for the purpose of creating a base to compare Values in the market, not to dictate pricing. However, to start we need to get prices in dollars in every national currency of our base items around the world to contribute to the price comparisons that calculate commodity Values.

We can use the McDonald's hamburger as an example (economists call this the "Big Mac Index"). If the hamburger is relatively the same in Jamaica as it is in America, and if most people know what a McDonalds hamburger is and about how much it costs in their community to buy one, then here we have a way to compare Values between communities. If the McDonald's hamburger is the same hamburger in the United States as in Jamaica but in Jamaica it costs $100 Jamaican dollars (JD) and the price in America is $1 (U.S. dollar [USD]) then we could use this as a base to believe that prices in Jamaica may be 100 times the prices in America. This means that the *relative Value*, or conversion rate for currency would be 1 USD = 100 JD. Just in case the hamburger is the price exception, it may be a more accurate comparison if we use a group or set of products for comparison. If we use a group of BHN items, then this may be a big enough group or sample set to generate a relative Value base that works for all people. It is proposed that we use this sample set (as listed in the Appendix). This information about the BHN items in this sample set and their relative Value is a currency. This currency is relative Value information about the market.

Markets feel like an elusive mystery when they do not have the information needed to discover Value. Value systems seem mysterious because the base Value of the dollar is manipulated and so, as a result, is almost every good and service on earth. The market feels elusive when we need to guess what our homes will be worth in the coming year. Capital markets are not efficient when companies need to guess how much food is needed and how many jeans to produce. Technology can give better Value information by collecting and comparing various dollar prices of BHN items all over the world. With a volume of dollar prices of these items then technology can use this information to make these items into commodities (similar items with known Value). The information of these items together can build a relative Value base.

This technology can also track the relative Value of dollars in different countries to what BHN those dollars can buy. From this base of Value, we can build relative Value to every other thing on earth. This technology will allow us to see that our labor, our land, and what we produce has intrinsic Value and will allow markets to find it. This information is currency.

The Problem of Differing Standards

The way to capitalize is to create comparables. When we can compare the Values of basic items in various currencies then we can see the percentage variations. If we can get a sample set of enough items to compare, then we can have an appropriate statistical base for that percentage variation calculation. This type of standardization can allow the world to speak the same Value language.

In its essence, Value language is about comparables, or differing standards. To break that down even further, it is about what is, and is not the same, at the same time. When we use the word "house" in English, the standard would be a structure to live in, but the idea includes some very different forms. When we use the word "coffee" we refer to a standard of bean, processed differently with many different tastes around the world. The term "comparable" is specifically used to describe the Valuation of a standard asset that is at once the same but different and so it can be used to mark a similar Value between two assets.

As you may remember from a mention earlier in the book, in real estate the term "comparable" is the English word often used to determine

Value by an appraiser of a house or property. The appraiser looks at more recently sold homes in a neighborhood as a standard for Value, even though the homes are different. The specific home being appraised is then adjusted from that Value based on the few differences. Comparables are a language of relative Value where standards are determined, and then relative differences used to arrive at Value. In this same way, items and services can be capitalized (assigned Value) for markets. The term "Value," again, as used in this thesis, is not necessarily equal to price. Free markets determine prices based on Value information.

The idea of differing standards as applied to a new base of Value is quite important. Given that coffee, rice, and canned tuna are included in the set of BHN, for example, each item (standard) will have differences around the world. The decision of what differences are acceptable per item (standard) is akin to the pronunciation of a word. The word may mean the same thing but may sound very different in the south part of a nation versus the north, or in the city versus the country. If coffee is Turkish or Blue Mountain or Rwandan, it may have different tastes and prices around the world. Coffee may be labeled in pounds or in grams or be packaged in square packs or in bags. The coffee may be branded Nestle or Folgers with different barcodes. But when we consider this item standard and the differences, we need to intentionally lose some specificity and back-up to discover a commodity perspective on the item. A tin of tuna, or "can of tuna," may be in water or oil, it may be Starkist or Chicken of the Sea, it may be Albacore or not, and the tin size may vary just a bit from country to country, or from store to store. Rice may be bagged or boxed or in a jar. It may be white rice or yellow or brown. The differing standards are not a problem when they are intentionally used to compare capital Values in order to build a language of Value.

Value data about the standard items is more dependable as the sample sets grow. The size of the "sample set" is a bit of economic-speak about the quantity of data for statistical analysis. This means that the more Value information that is gathered about the standard item—rice, for example— the more we can depend on the data. It is possible to chart what Values occur most of the time, and what Values are outliers. It is possible to mathematically give more weight, or more attention, to Values that occur more often, such as by using a weighted average. The idea of a "sample set" of

100 reports of the retail price of rice in Puerto Rico would not be nearly as effective as 1,000 reports about rice in Puerto Rico. The bigger the sample set, the less impact the differences make as they are averaged together.

This is the very reason that it is important to have a set of BHN to defy the problem of just one or two item standards. It is also the reason that we need to depend on more than one category of BHN, such as food, building materials, paper, clothes, and medical/hygiene supplies. With this variation of items and categories, which together represent basic needs, we can have confidence in our sample set for a base of Value. All of the items in the sample set can be compared by nation, even with unique, different dollar currencies. The reason that this is possible is because the focus has changed from the dollars being the currency to the tuna, a coffee, and the rice being the currency. The information about how much the tuna costs in dollars is no longer considered information about real Value. The market needs information about how much the dollars cost in tuna. How many euros will the coffee buy? How many pesos will the rice buy? And with our total sample set of BHN, we will want to know: How many sets of BHN will the dollar buy in the United States? How many sets of BHN will the peso buy in Argentina? How many sets of BHN will the rand buy in South Africa? It is possible to use ratios to compare these sample sets of BHN. These ratios can then operate as dollar conversions between countries.

This confidence in a common standard of Value will enable the next iteration of Value language, which is the capitalization of other items and services based on their relative Value to this standard translator, or this comparable. The new information currency is a language of comparables based on the Values of a standard set of BHN.

When we achieve multilingual Value independence from dollar language by operating confidently in a new standard of Value then we will achieve a new freedom. In this new civilization, Value will be relative to our humanity as compared to a world where our Value is depreciated by dollars.

Will We Always Need Dollars?

We will always be obligated to "Give to Caesar what is Caesar's" and most governments will require that we pay taxes in dollars.

New Value languages will mitigate the Greatest Deception. Armed with an index that can show relative Value of dollars to a base of Value, it is possible to show more realistic dollar exchange rates than the FOREX. With a base of Value, we will also be able to detect a declining Value of dollars to our BHN.

Item Banc technology was used to run an initial test in 2020 to show the relative Value of dollars to a base of 14 basic items in 26 countries. The relative Value data was used to create exchange rates between the 26 countries to the USD using the base of items. These exchange rates using the set of items were compared to the FOREX rates to the USD. The result was that for 21 of the 26 countries paired to the USD, the FOREX calculated the USD exchange more than significantly stronger than by comparing the relative cost of the 14 basic items in the countries tested. This difference is documented in the test mentioned on the last line of the spreadsheet data included (refer pages 153 to 155). Using the FOREX for exchange then creates a situation that makes it harder for developing countries when the USD is strong (very expensive), and for the United States this makes imported goods cheaper.

FOREX rates tell the story of the market for dollar traders. This market is speculative, profit-driven, and a zero-sum game. The story behind the relative Value of BHN is grounded and specifically answers the need for a Value base that tells the truth about what matters to most humans. Prior to the dawn of the Internet and free information, and prior to the blockchain revolution, we did not have the technology or freedom to decide about what to use for a base of Value. Now we can achieve the goal to use information as currency. By moving through this paradigm shift, dollar Values will be defined outside of the FOREX traders' and the central banks' game. Likely we will use dollars and many other forms of currency, but we will have the technology to not be deceived about their relative Value. Our currency will be information and we will not be alone with or held hostage to dollars much longer.

We will not need dollars as often, but we will continue to speak dollar language for years to come. In cryptocurrency, there is a natural need to represent dollar language. To simulate this, the traders in crypto have created Tether (USDT) and USDC. These are cryptocurrencies that are not issued by governments but represent the dollar language. USDT is owned and issued by Bitfinex, and USDC is open-source, and managed by members of Circle and Coinbase. Other representations or names for dollars used in decentralized finance include Maker Dao (DAI) which also uses dollar language. Some digital "dollars" like the Yuan are being issued directly by China. This new information language is also currency, and since most of society was raised in dollar languages, we will naturally remember how we first learned to speak Value. Dollars will likely continue as our first language.

CHAPTER 3

Technology for Our New Value Language

Information Currency Technologies

We need to use new technology to develop a new Value language. It can help people, companies, and economies become more efficient and stable. Information becomes currency if we can combine the barter functions of the past with technology that we can use today. This section of the book tells the story of how this is becoming real.

The *first* new concept to understand with new Value technology is that with dollars we use one word for Value and in our new language technology we use many words. Think about it in the same way you would approach a serious effort to enlarge your vocabulary.

To start thinking this way, imagine that you won a lottery ticket for a Jeep. That ticket represents the Jeep, ownership of the Jeep, and the Value of the Jeep all at once. Technology has new types of tickets that are digital, and what is special about these tickets is that they are encrypted with a secret and private number called a key. It makes sense that if you had a ticket for a Jeep, especially if it was digital (on your phone or your computer), that you would want to make sure it was secure. These digitally encrypted tickets are called tokens. In this new technology, a Jeep token can represent the Value of a real Jeep. This Jeep token is now a new word in your Value vocabulary. For instance, if asked about the Value of a red Jeep in the parking lot you would not say dollars followed by a number, you would just say "Jeep" followed by the specifications of that vehicle. The technology can tokenize a specific type of Jeep so the vehicle itself is a symbol or ticket of Value.

A *second* example of token Value language is a token that represents a service. A token for accounting services, for instance, could represent the

Value of preparing tax returns or an hourly Value of accounting work by a professional. If you held that token, then it becomes the Value of and the ticket for that service. A token can be a ticket for a hotel stay. A token can be like a gift card to shop at a store or a token can be a dinner at a Mexican restaurant.

A *third* concept is that markets are being redefined in the new Value language. When you go to market now, you go to a store, whether physically or online. When you go shopping in this new technology, you will be able to create the store and everything in it. For example, if you shop for socks, it will be as if you enter a virtual catalog of every sock available and you can edit the styles down to the specifics you need because the socks are tokenized as items available, and their source is secondary. In the near future you will also be able to shop as an avatar, or representation of you, in virtual, 3-dimensional worlds that are named the Metaverse.

For the *fourth* shocking concept, in the new language of Information Currency almost all Values are known or are easily discoverable. Values are relative to other things, but of course, you can always revert to dollar translations. If we want to acquire a Jeep today in dollar world, we need to call around or go visit places to get a price to make a deal. In our new technology, the Values of things will be connected and accessible and relevant because all things (items and services) will have independent tokenized identities that are discoverable and comparable on the blockchain highway, like a big Amazon.

The *fifth* language technology makes transactions direct and secure. Dollar language transactions first must translate to dollars then often must transact through a bank. In new transaction technologies, cryptography is used to secure the tokenized Value and the transaction directly from one party to another. A token can be sent to or assigned easily to a new person if the token secret key holder allows the transaction. The Jeep token holder can send or assign that Jeep to anyone. The person who has Mexican meal tokens can transact with the holder of accounting tokens.

A *sixth* language change is that the Value technology will assign things to an entity instead of transferring Value to dollars. With tech that can assign and encrypt an identity for you and your business, it then becomes simple to assign other tokenized assets, or representations of Value, to you and to any entity. Imagine a metal poster of you on the wall with a magnet attached that looks like every asset that you own. The magnet that looks like a car may be stuck on you, maybe a magnet for a house or a lawnmower, a computer, a phone, or a TV. There may be a magnet that represents U.S. dollars too. You may also have a magnet that represents the work that you will do this month. That work you can do, that capacity, is an asset that can be capitalized using a token. Each magnet can be represented as a distinct token assigned to you. Each magnet assigned to you is one that you can transfer or assign to someone else. Tokens are new words for our Value language. Tokens represent the new Information Currency.

Sovereignty for every entity is the *seventh* opportunity for those who speak the language of Information Currency. The people, organizations, and companies who use this new technology language will experience a new sovereignty over their own Value.

The discussion going forward is about how technology is making information a currency and how you can learn to use and benefit from this Value language. But first we need to look at the massive change happening to information about prices in dollars as technology removes the veils that have mystified price discovery.

Oracles of Prices and Relative Value Truth

When we can know what is available where and at what relative Value then business can become more efficient for everyone in the world. We now have technology that can move this data language and secure real-time information for asset Values and transactions. We can use a technology tool like the Item Banc Index that can create relative Value information about assets based on volumes of data that can be secured, compared, and verified around the world instantly. As we have mentioned before, the digital currency and blockchain industry names these streams of data validators "oracles."

Imagine a world where prices stream like movies … where the "what is available where at what Value" was like a Google search where you could see a ticker tape rolling on your screen for any product at any time anywhere. This is hard to foresee because prices still feel like company or industry secrets. Times have changed and almost all prices will soon come out of their closets.

Times changed in the 1990s when the Internet threatened business models and competitive landscapes. Internet technology changed the entire distribution industry when many prices were published.

The next wave of massive change is here as the technology of oracles can move real-time prices out of siloed websites and businesses, and siloed salesmen's lairs onto Internet-based blockchain highways where prices are free and available information. The technologies of oracles such as Chainlink, Band, DOS, and others are integrating real-world, real-time price streams onto blockchains. For now, think of block-chains as permanent memories of the sequential order and details of transactions on the Internet that are available to everyone. Big business systems such as SAP (a multinational software company known for its Enterprise Resource Planning [ERP] software) can use Baseline technology built by Unibright to attach legacy information systems to on- and off-ramp data.[1] As the legacy systems integrate their own requisition and inventory systems, they can simultaneously have this data moved externally to trade partners on the blockchain without sacrificing internal data. This inventory, production, and price data is moving along potentially even faster than the Internet itself did. The result will be that what capital is available where and the relative Value of everything will soon be known.

Oracles which stream prices of products around the world will allow us to see the relative truth about product prices in any dollar currency anywhere. We will be able to stream the price of eggs in U.S. dollars in every state. We may be able to stream the prices of eggs in Euros in France or in China with Yuan.

This seems like the tower of Babel—the Old Testament story of how many languages started—because we will have price information about every item to compare in every dollar currency. Our Value language will need an interpreter. We can use the tools that we have for currency exchange, which are data-based on those who buy and sell currencies, or we can work to discover the revealing truth about the relative Value of currencies. This will in turn give us the truth about the relative Value of products. We can feed product price data into a technology engine that compares and interprets various dollar languages about the same items so that we can know the truth about their relative Value.

It is now possible to create a base of relative Value from the items that every human needs. We will examine this question again and a way to move forward.

Moving to Rational Equilibrium

Real-time availability (quantity) and relative Value information (prices) about BHN items around the world can introduce a new base for market equilibrium.

The "trickle-up" of market data about basic human need (BHN) items around the world allows the market to find rational equilibrium. Rational equilibrium will be reached when the balance of weighted averages of quantities and prices of BHN items around the world become widely known. The rational equilibrium reached from the set of these products can establish the floor, or invariant, used for Value. From this base of Value, the market can then relate other products and services and then reach their fair market Value as well, similar to the way comparables work.

To accomplish this "trickle-up" data feed of the available quantity and prices of BHN items around the world, we will need to use a common base of naming systems used across nations and with a necessary and limited category set for BHN items. The technology needs to understand that the BHN item "lumber," for instance, is also called "wood" in some countries. A "can" of tuna is the same as a "tin" of tuna. Then, of course, it is necessary to integrate words in other languages, like "las maderas" (the Spanish term for "lumber"). When the Values of these items become widely known and their Value widely translated and correlated, the items will transform into commodities. Commodities have shown to have market power in that they prove relative Value within markets, and if used as a common base for comparison, can lead external markets toward rational equilibrium also. This ticker tape of real-time data feeds will be recorded on the blockchain as a trusted, permanent record for the world to see. Now this data feed about price and availability of basic needed products can become the floor that the markets can stand on.

The new commodity data for markets will bring small business some efficiency that only large corporations have had in the past. Small business can use this data to know what prices are competitive. Consumers can know the fair market Values of what they need. International markets can be informed by the fair market Value of goods and services that each nation brings to the world. This is possible when a common base of Value is used to bring rational equilibrium to markets.

The rational equilibrium for currency is derived from a common base of information about what is available, where it is, and at what relative Value. This information is also the market. More complete and comparable information about the market becomes the currency. Then the information is currency.

Babel begone!

The Technology That Beats the Babel Problem

The Babel Problem is that the Value languages we speak need an interpreter. A technology that focuses on delivering the BHN Value index to market is Item Banc. This blockchain-interactive technology design offers a starting point to acquire prices of Basic Need products in markets all over the world. The technology reports their relative Value language (translation) standards to the blockchain. The Item Banc Index will allow the world to translate Value languages and to subsequently capitalize the market.

In case you put the book down for a moment, the Babel Problem is that the Value languages we speak need an interpreter. A technology that focuses on delivering the BHN Value set to market is Item Banc. This blockchain-interactive technology design offers a starting point for acquiring and comparing the prices of BHN products in markets around the world and reports the relative Value language that is needed to capitalize the market for Information Currency.

Let's see exactly how that works using an example.

Gift cards are a good example of how this technology can function in real markets. Initially, it may appear that gift cards are denominated in U.S. dollars but behind the curtain is the real fact that gift cards are NOT U.S. dollars. A gift card represents a specific set of capital in goods or services from a merchant. If a gift card holder wants to turn that card back into dollars, he or she will receive fewer dollars than were originally used to purchase the card. Companies like CardCash.com calculate the relative Value of the gift card capital to dollars and then publish it on the

Internet. This capitalization process commoditizes the goods or services for market in dollars. The technology we need for Information Currency needs to be able to trade gift card for gift card—capital for capital. This is a prime example of functioning Information Currency. In this context, liquidity is just the ability to exchange a Value item or service anytime for anything. A method is needed to simplify the exchange of capital for capital (one gift card for another) by making assignment and transfer of the Value item easier.

Value assignment and transfer can work with gift-card-like crypto tokens if they can be backed by (or Valued by) the available capital of basic needed products. For example, if one person had a gift card for a hardware store, and a second person had a gift card for a computer supplier, and a third person had a gift card for airline miles it may not always be easy to transfer between them. For example, the person who had the computer gift card may not need airline miles. If, however, all the cards were backed by, or redeemable at the local Walmart (which sells many BHN products), then all the gift cards would be more liquid. This means that if you wanted to trade your airline miles gift card to buy pizza, the pizza owner would be happy to take it as it would be backed by an easily redeemable Walmart card, and the Value of that card would be connected directly to the Values of what items are available at the Walmart store.

A technology that represents the Value information of basic, needed items can be used as a translator for a Value decision for other items. Banks, finance, and capital markets can move to the next level of Information Currency when they can define the Value of items and companies with a relative Value index like Item Banc, which then can provide relative Value broadly to markets. If lenders understood the basic Value of markets by person, by company, by city, and by country then they would be able to loan for growth.

Information about relative Value is currency. This new currency can build new capital markets for the world.

Value Validators

Data about what Basic Needs items are available, where they are, and at what price they're available can "trickle up." People can record local prices into their smartphone or computer on the specific set of

BHN items and can be rewarded with tokens. They will also be able to see this information recorded by others.

These price Validators can grow into communities that contribute to a social purpose to "trickle up" the data needed to create a base floor of Value for the market.

Validators can be rewarded with tokens for recording the information, and these tokens then can be spent by users for regional price information about the complete set of BHN goods. In the most preferred setup, the data is organized by country to send real-time retail prices and available quantity on any item in the specific set of BHN items to a distributed blockchain for the user-entered data.

From this floor of data, Item Banc technology can derive and publish relative Valuation, like a new kind of exchange rate for dollar currencies. The Item Banc can take in the real-time data from the Validators to compare the Value of these BHN baskets of Value by country, using algorithms similar to the economic concept of Purchasing Power Parity. The Item Banc contributes to setting a standard for Information Currency, where the relative Value of a basic set of needed goods contributes to the Valuation of other currencies and other products from a base Value floor.

Currently, this market supply information (what BHN items are available, where they are, and at what price they're available) moves from manufacturers and distributors then back up from their connected retailers. This vital market data is kept within these relationships. Outside customers are shut out. Outside suppliers, manufacturers, and markets in other cities are shut out. Outside countries are shut out. Not only that, but alternative, substitute products, with slightly different packaging are also shut out of these markets. It has become conventional wisdom to accept this market situation for business and rely on the random work of product salesmen or the overtures of aggressive purchasing agents.

Platforms like Alibaba have taken advantage this market fault by opening outside suppliers to business buyers. Amazon has also discovered success as well by directing retail customers to a wide array of outside suppliers.

Markets will open and fill up like oceans when new information is made available about what basic needed items are available, where, and at what price. This information in turn becomes the basis for a language of relative Value that the whole world can understand. This information is currency.

Market Demand for Price Information

The current industry and consumer demand for market price information and the spread of product commoditization is the catalyst for an increasing market expectation for information about what is available, where it is located, and at what Value. With this information corporations will capitalize their production and establish relative Values to market.

An indicator of the natural movement toward Information Currency is the demand for price information that is leading to increased commoditization of products. For example, before a purchase a consumer will spend time searching comparable prices for an item. Before the Internet, shoppers had to physically go to a store or a mall to discover the price of a product. Now shoppers take for granted the search engines that easily display product price information; Google and Amazon are used to compare prices to find the Value of a product. Products and services are commoditized (discovered and Valued as similar items) behind the scenes in software code that understand that a vacuum cleaner is the same as a Hoover. Market Value (commodity Value) of a turmeric tea or a package of Oreo cookies can be discovered easily. This shift in software technology was developed on purpose as industry discovered that there was power in creating a known relative Value for their products.

In the systems management echelons of retail, wholesale distribution, and manufacturing, there has been a movement to standardize product data, naming, and categorization systems. One of the early pioneers was Trade Service, dating back to 1931 when their pricing "pages" were passed around the industry. Trade Service is still a product pricing technology leader in the electrical, hardware, and industrial equipment industries. The corporation, in friendly competition with IDEA (IDW), makes a living communicating product data along the supply chain primarily in the electrical industry. The concept of "standard" or "market" cost has bled into many other industries. This concept is the foundational thinking for Information Currency and the movement just keeps improving with technology.

The demand for market price information, specifically toward "standard" commoditized product pricing is also leveraged in many industries. For example, lumber distributors use the services of the company Random Lengths (www.randomlengths.com) to provide market Value weekly for sheet goods such as plywood and lumber. From this weekly market price, these dealers establish their market pricing for the week. Random Lengths sources prices of lumber from all over the world to commoditize lumber products.

The current industry and consumer demand for market price information and the spread of product commoditization is the catalyst for an increasing market expectation for information about what is available, where it is, and at what Value it is available. With this information, corporations can capitalize their production and establish relative Values to market. This information capital is currency. It has intrinsic Value.

Capitalizing Information

The world can regenerate Value if we capitalize Value information by representing assets digitally in tokens and assigning these tokenized assets to entities. It begins with businesses, where the stocked inventory information is tokenized and logged on an open blockchain. This declares to the market what is available, where it is located, and at what Value in real time. It begins when meals offered by restaurants have public tokenized Value. It also begins when manufacturers directly instruct the market about what they have already produced by tokenizing the assets. Even service providers such as contractors can show quantified Value of services available at market Value in token form.

It is possible to capitalize information in the same way that legal title to land and buildings are used to make capital? Some economists contend that it is the formalizing of legal title to capital that differentiates the first from the third world. It is this efficient legal set that empowers banks and other venture partners to loan. If the third world could create these efficient legal sets to allow businesses to capitalize on land and building assets then some believe the third world, with dead capital Valued at over $9 trillion, might no longer be third world.

—Hernando Desoto, *The Mystery of Capital*[2]

In the Wild West a cowboy might have staked out and claimed a piece of land near a town and farmed wheat. Based on the assignment of the asset of land and the commodity Value of wheat, he secured the relative Value of his production for the community. In other words, the farmer was able to capitalize on the Value information related to assets assigned to him and use this leverage to barter in that community.

We will be able to leverage and weave the Values in communities and nations together if we capitalize them by structuring Value information and by assigning these tokenized assets to entities. It begins with business entities, where the stocked inventory information is declared together with the world market of similar items, where they are available and at what Value. It begins when menus made available by restaurants have tokenized Value to a community even before a hungry customer is served. It also begins when manufacturers are directly instructed by the market about what needs to be produced. This new market begins when service providers such as contractors, teachers, and truck drivers can identify and issue their services with a specific Value definition that locates their markets nearby. The Value of labor to communities can be tokenized and woven together by a new form of union that publishes the Value of like services and leverages them together in the world.

Items are dead capital if the market does not have direct access to information about them. When we fail to leverage information as capital, we follow the third world in the failure to leverage dead stock, land, and buildings. Creating capital from information is practiced in retail barter economies. A retail barter exchange capitalizes businesses and service providers by offering to market the information about what is available, where it is located, and what is its Value. The barter industry specializes in capitalizing Value information of nonproductive assets.

Assets need to be defined and assigned digitally. This simply means that what specific inventory or services in what amount and where they are available to market need to be tokenized and assigned to a company or person. In order to move on to leverage these assets as capital, they need this information structure. This truth is evidenced by the monumental success of Alibaba and Amazon.

The process of methodically structuring and publishing Value assignments using new blockchain technologies will be the process that capitalizes Information Currency.

Entry Into the New Space

It is evident that this new Information Currency language has some similarities to barter but it can create millions more markets, can connect opportunities faster, can function in massive transactions, and can completely capitalize markets. Comparing barter to Information Currency is like comparing the social network possible in a small town 30 years ago to the scope of the social network of Facebook or LinkedIn.

In this new space you can see every market "face" because every market maker will have a place. If for an example, we revert to the Western town and implement Information Currency, we would begin by identifying every potential market maker and assigning each one a virtual entity market "face." In this space, everyone in town would be able to see your "face" so to speak, and each "face" would be catalogued with a Key. The market maker chicken farm would get a virtual number key that would represent the Western town chicken farm's "face." A worker on the chicken farm would get a number key that represented chicken maker labor. The general store would get a new "face" and so would Western town doctor "face."

In a far-Eastern town, the market "faces" most likely would have doctor "faces," general store "faces," chicken farm "faces," and chicken maker labor "faces" too. In this new technology space, the "faces" are built to relate. So soon all around the world the market makers mix similar "faces" and these similar virtual "face" representations of market makers together construct new economies and the opportunities to scale. This is how millions of new markets can be made.

With millions of markets come millions more products and services that can relate and are made to virtually trade. An Eastern town doctor has plenty to offer, like flu shots and broken arm slings, and so does Western doctor, as everyone knows his flu shots, arm slings and other, more specific, cowboy things such as hats and saddles. Now the record can show flu shots and slings wherever you go. Enter this virtual market and you can see the automated market maker transactions shown as possible become likely and then they can close.

Millions more transactions will be likely as a result of new information parlayed, related, and relayed perfectly. This option is new because of the encryption guru (Satoshi). Now virtual "faces" can safely parlay on world spaces. Similar products and services (like Uniswap) can be virtually related but not taken over by using Baseline structures (Unibright). Now chains of events are secured (Ethereum), and are made and relayed with no dollars denominated.

The capital has always been there for markets, but old technology did not see it. Old technology did not share it. Old technology did not compare it. Information Currency (the new technology) makes markets more aware. It has the ability to share and compare and so the capital will be there. You can enter all capital possible in this space to ensure there is no information waste. Take no time to be confused and wait. Just enter and practice making your capital safe and accept the urgency to build Information Currency.

CHAPTER 4

Making the Switch to an Information Currency

Will There Be Standardization?

The age of one world reserve currency such as a U.S. dollar standard has now transformed into a situation that looks a lot more like the Tower of Babel where, in the story, suddenly the world was cursed and went from one language to many, and the people were confused and frightened and could not communicate.

The world is evolving away from the U.S. dollar (USD) as a standard. Like Babel, with a new plethora of crypto and digital currencies, we can choose to become confused and frightened at the fact that one dollar standard is no longer working, or we can choose to embrace the change and redefine the kind of standard that is needed. As discussed, we need to answer the question about what base of Value we should use. This book proposes a base that includes basic human needs (BHN). With this, there is no need for one world currency reserve but instead an index of BHN related to all currencies that can be used as an interpreter to create relative Value of all currencies.

What needs to be standardized is *first*, the BHN product set; *second*, the methods to trickle up price information; *third*, the naming systems of these basic products; *fourth*, implementation of an Item Banc index into the financial sector; and finally, *fifth*, the backing of governments and businesses.

Crypto Adoption by Banks and Finance

Bitcoin was force-fed to banks by businesses who were front-runners of the technology. Now in the United States, the Comptroller of the

Currency (OCC) declared that banks should offer custodial services for their customer's private crypto keys. This type of crypto adoption is happening in banks for major crypto currencies such as Bitcoin and Ethereum (ETH) around the world. But banks and financial institutions will need to integrate new tools to convert an entire set of crypto currencies and dollars. In addition, as Value languages interact with finance, it will be critical for banks to have a standard to use for comparables as asset Valuation for loans. But most critical is the approaching reality that banks and financial institutions may be dinosaurs in their current form and may not adapt very well to the Tower of Babel-like currency cluster that is incoming.

Let us set up the Babel-bank problem. In this scenario, barter exchange houses will be compared to banks in different countries. The goal will be to understand the problem in order to understand the urgent need for standardization.

Using an example in the barter industry, imagine a barter exchange in New York with 200 businesses that are members. The New York exchange has its own currency that circulates between the business members. Then imagine a similar barter exchange in Atlanta with about 100 members and their own circulating currency as well. If a member of the New York exchange wanted to trade with a member of the Atlanta exchange, what currency would he or she use? Relate this scenario to a bank in Jamaica with a customer who wants to do business with a customer of a bank in Miami. What currency would they use? Would they use the Jamaican dollars or the USD? What has been tradition is to use USD and the conversion determined by FOREX as a base for Value comparison.

A similar solution is worked out in the barter world. The Atlanta exchange can trade with the New York exchange by each converting their specific currencies into what is named Universal Currency (UC). The UC is USD-based as well. What happens when this base that the world has used for relative Value, the USD, is debased? With price inflation, it will take more USD to buy other currencies and products. In other words, as the dollar is printed and minted into infinity, so its relative Value to other currencies may no longer be considered stable. This shift is monumental to the world as this dollar paradigm may be sinking.

A standard for Value in banking and barter is required. If the USD is not a standard of Value, what can the banks use? As many banks are incorporating Bitcoin and ETH custody and transactions, it would be possible to consider one of these as an elective standard. But in the real world, both of these would strangle Value languages. This is because neither Bitcoin nor ETH are normally used as money in daily life. Bitcoin is hoarded like gold. ETH's Value is mostly used for token creation and as a blockchain base layer to auto-function programs for new technologies like decentralized finance (DeFi). ETH has not been commonly used to buy products and services.

Banks and financial institutions need to adopt new methods to translate Value languages across the world. To solve the incoming Babel problem where dollar Values are disrupted and cannot be trusted and with many Value languages (dollar and cryptocurrencies) to translate, banks will need a solution. One option is to use technology like Item Banc for Value language discovery and multicurrency exchange.

With the realization that existing technology can make information currency comes a responsibility to define what our base of Value should be. When we decide this, banks will follow, and our information will be currency.

Adoption by Governments and Government Agencies

Governments can have greater economic security by building information about the capital available to market in their country for Information Currency. This market information can be used for leverage in the global economy and can assist in the efficiency of national economies.

It is possible to invert the historical pattern of central banks minting currency without backing and then forwarding it to selected players in the financial system. As an alternative, with the direction of governments, a central bank could issue CBDC (Central Bank Digital Currencies) to capital owners based on the true Value of the represented capital as tokenized by the owners of the goods and services. With this alternative, national governments can build an entirely new system for Value leverage and exchange that is ready to go.

How does this begin?

The nation must begin with the capitalization of BHN. This data forms the foundation for a Value base. With Validators on the ground who can report what BHN items are available for retail, in what quantity, where they are, and at what price, the BHN can be capitalized. A national government can further capitalize, as later outlined in this book, by incenting all companies to tokenize the detail of the on-hand inventories of all products to capitalize national production. Service organizations and individuals can tokenize their available capital by specialty. The government can incentivize the tokenization of capital by providing loans in exchange for the inventory and service information of the companies and individuals, and then would mint currency to match the reported capital Values. This Information Currency would secure Value to items and services and these building blocks of Value structure would collateralize and capitalize a nation.

An analogy to this method is how a barter exchange issues trade currency based on the Value of the goods and available services of its members. If an exchange had 100 members, each would be issued trade currency to start equal to the Value of the goods and services offered into the exchange. For instance, the Mexican restaurant may get $2,000 in currency for offering to provide 100 meals for $20 each. A lawyer member may get $400 in the trade currency for offering two consulting sessions. The dentist member may get $10,000 of the currency for one hundred patient visits. A contractor member may be issued $1,000 for committing 10 hours of labor to the exchange, and the computer store may be issued $5,000 by the exchange for providing five computers on trade. The grocery store member may allow all bakery items on trade for a total of $500. The barter economy in this example would more immediately give rise to transactions and sustain a balance for trade.

If instead the exchange operated like the way that the central banks currently work, then they would issue a random amount of trade currency on a random time basis to only about five of the 100 members. It would be as if the exchange only gave credit of $1,000 each to five lawyer-members randomly two times a year. The 95 members would have no ability to trade until one of the five premier members spent some of their trade dollars either directly with them or indirectly through another member that then decided to trade with them. A similar kind of capital misdirection occurs through central banks into nations.

If a nation capitalizes with Information Currency, then the information capital can also be properly published, and the nation can organically organize more efficient market behavior. Capital markets can function most efficiently with open information about what is available, where it is, and at what Value. Though conventional wisdom may regard Information about goods and services available to markets as a private (as opposed to public) good, and though some citizens and companies may consider it a benefit to keep certain market information secret to maximize profits, this occurs at the expense of market efficiency.

As an analogy in a barter exchange economy, some trade exchanges are known to keep the best trade members and offerings a secret so that the best trade can be consumed by the owners of the trade exchange. If the best restaurants, lawyers, dentist services, contractors, and computer equipment, for instance, are kept secret and consumed by the owners of the exchange then there is, by default, less motivation for existing members to trade and less incentive for new members to join that barter economy. In this example, these best trade options are information capital that the barter exchange did not properly publish and make available to their market.

There is a massive benefit to a nation to properly capitalize and publish goods and services. This nation can affect such economies of scale, and these macro benefits of bringing information capital to markets have been made evident by Amazon and Alibaba. The Amazon business model primarily capitalizes information organized by product about what suppliers are available, where they (and the products) are, and at what price they are available to a retail market. The Alibaba model primarily capitalizes information organized by category and product about what suppliers are available, where they are, and at what price they are available to a wholesale or business market. These business models demonstrate the power, profitability, and global demand for Information about what is available where at what Value.

The goods and services available to market are of significant Value to all nations. This information can be asked of their business owners, and then rewarded in a CBDC by the nation for the public good. If the ownership of assets such as homes and cars by individuals, and buildings and machines by corporations is considered information required for the purpose of taxation (a rather negative incentive), then certainly creating an incentive to collect and publish national information capital for the public good seems rational.

A plan for information currency, as discussed in this book, would provide a new economic advantage to all of society. Nations can build Item Bancs, infrastructure, exchange systems, management rules, and security systems. Nations can be ready with new technology for currency that could lift it out of an apparent dead end. With this plan, currency-challenged nations can build a new economic order. Governments can give tax incentives for private companies to build the technologies that structure information currency (such as integrating the Value floor, the reference of base Value like the first floor of a building) for BHN items using Item Banc. This reference of Value can operate as the new comparable to other products and services. These technologies would bring the information about capital—what is available, where it is, and at what Value—into the markets by rewarding those who bring in new data.

The impact of harnessing product and service Value and availability information that is captured, capitalized, commoditized, and secured is that this super-productive information currency instrument allows us to effect transactions with this data. The technology of an information currency will bring back rational equilibrium to markets and create an economic insurance policy against currency failure. This success will happen when the nation's currency is the synthetic representation of market information and then its information market will transform into currency.

Should You Wait for Standardization of Value?

Technology has finally reached a place where the implementation of an Information Currency is possible because the standards are in place for us to speak the language.

The technology components necessary for a language of Value using Information Currency include an ability to communicate information for free (like a virtual voice to speak), a way to make permanent records for transactions in time (similar to a written language), a way to create a secure virtual entity (like having an identity as the speaker), and a way to make a synthetic, virtual representation of everything on earth (like the representation of words for things and ideas) using blockchain technology.

The Internet allows for virtually free information transfer. From the moment that this technology was created and became public on August 6, 1991, the possibility of an Information Currency was born. This is because information is currency and currency is information.

With the technology of Bitcoin in 2008, we were able to create immutable records of transactions on the blockchain. This ability to make permanent records of Value exchange creates order in a Value language in a similar way that a written language orders a verbal language. The records of transactions on the Bitcoin blockchain are accessible for anyone to read any transaction. The account numbers are recorded without names which can allow for anonymity, but the permanence creates evidence. The methods of transaction do not require trust between parties so the result is that this Value language can be spoken to anyone, at anytime, anywhere. These accounts are encrypted and the holder who has the key can choose anonymity; however, regulators work against this choice requiring Know Your Customer (KYC) rules. A new entity movement going forward is converting from numbered accounts to named and numbered accounts assigned to companies, organizations, and individuals.

Vitalik Buterin was inspired in 2015 to create ETH, which was the first layer of a technical standard for a blockchain that would allow the creation of tokens that could synthetically represent anything or any idea on earth. Now what is left to create and standardize are basically the "words" in our Value language. As an analogy, it is like the world needs to provide the information "words" about what is available and where. Each "word" needs to be created as a token. There is an urgent need for everyone and every company in the world that has something to offer or sell to create their items or services on this kind of "free world Amazon." In addition, every person and company in the world will need to create an identity, or they cannot speak and be heard. In order to speak this language of Value, we all need to make a synthetic representation of ourselves (we all need a name) and a word (or token) for everything on this earth ... just like a language. These words are spoken on blockchains. Many industries have their own chains. These chains are becoming interoperable (basically tokens can work or be exchanged on any blockchain no matter which one they originated on), so their groups can speak together, and the Values and token "words" can move or be spoken anywhere in the world to any entity. This is the freedom and power of Information Currency.

But without a standard of Value these words shouted everywhere evoke chaos. This new standard base such as the proposed relative Value of a set of BHN must be considered, or our freedom will bring us straight back to the city of Babel.

The Opportunity Cost of Waiting

We have an opportunity to capitalize on information about what is available, where it is, and at what Value. We can wait but why do that? Economies will become more efficient and business benefits greatly.

The Value language of Information Currency is an opportunity to capitalize, advertise, and monetize.

A traditional way to understand how to capitalize a business is to add assets. The business could add money to its bank account, purchase inventories, buy a new machine to manufacture, acquire a delivery truck, or even add human capital such as technical specialties on staff. The new opportunity is like this but instead of just *acquiring* assets to capitalize, the business needs to *define* its assets as information capital. In a similar method to adding items for sale on Alibaba or Amazon, the business needs to tokenize its products or services so that the Value of the assets available to market can be capitalized, advertised, and monetized as synthetic virtual assets.

Once tokenized as a synthetic and virtual representation of what is real, the digital asset can go on the chain and based on its definition, can be easily discovered worldwide by universal languages that connect similar tokens, or "words" for things using the blockchain "sentences" as structure for the explorer. The tokens can represent a set of similar items. In this case, each token is the same, or fungible. For instance, the tokens could represent an available service, such as a meal at a restaurant or a service-in-time like painting by the hour. A token can also represent a unique item like a work of art, a unique truck, or a specific house. This kind is called nonfungible token, or NFT, a term we have previously introduced.

Tokens can be sold and exchanged anytime, almost anywhere in the world as they can be explored simply by similar "words" that relate and make them visible at market. Once seen, the tokens can be exchanged or monetized often with automated market makers (AMM) that operate like robots programmed to read the blockchain "sentences" to find relevant transactions and then automatically execute them. (Technically, the owners of the tokens need to agree to sell, and other owners of tokens need to agree to leverage their tokens, and the AMM is simply an algorithm that manages this.)

In addition to tokenizing items for sale, the business or individual can also capitalize by tokenizing (synthetically *defining*) other balance sheet assets. Each asset that is tokenized can be thought of like a new refrigerator magnet that has attached Value to the entity. By tokenizing balance sheet assets, a business or individual makes leverage to use for loans. There is more on DeFi to look forward to in following chapters. As you may remember from earlier in the book, DeFi is a method to leverage digital assets for finance using technology, and not banks or other corporate middlemen.

The cost of waiting to *define* assets in the form of tokens is a lost opportunity to capitalize into an Information Currency language that will advertise and monetize items and services to the world.

The Risks of Waiting

If we leverage information currency soon by capitalizing assets using tokenization, we will be able to increase the Value that we have worked so hard for by allowing these assets to be seen by the market.

By capitalizing ourselves as individuals and by capitalizing our businesses, we can enable Information Currency. Imagine if every business put every inventory item in the form of a token, and with this also attached every other balance sheet asset in the form of a token to a virtual, published, and digital entity. Imagine attaching every asset that you own in the form of a token. Imagine that in combination with this there existed a proper standard of Value. Then with this you have created a digital, synthetic image of you as an Entity of Value. This process of capitalization by tokenization along with an accepted standard of Value will completely revolutionize the economic efficiency of the world. With this ability to embody Value into our language, we can strategically unhinge our world from the need for a medium of exchange.

To embody Value directly into an entity we simply add the sum of its parts. A business Value is made up of the sum of its tokens of Value. A human Entity of Value is also equal to the sum of its tokens of Value. From here one can see an ability to revert to the ways of the Western barter town. In the Western town, the doctor takes eggs from the farm and there is trust that he will provide services later. The general store gives credit to the chicken farm for feed and then may take in trade some doctor services. Credit is moved directly from entity to entity. But everyone in the Western town knows everyone.

If Information Currency can capitalize entities and if these entities can exchange Value in a similar method to the Western town, then at the scale of the world this could demand that trust rise to an unmanageable level … or would it? We trust dollars knowing that their Value today is worth less than yesterday! But with the help of new technologies such as Bondly (https://bondly.finance) and Paid Network (https://paidnetwork.com) the contracts for exchange and debt relating to real physical goods can be managed with bonds and arbitrated using contract validating nodes.[1] Basically, these protocols work when counter-parties post a type of "bond" on the blockchain that is released when the participating, arbitrating nodes agree.

For every creditor in the Western town, there is a debtor. In a bartering economy, debt does not carry the zero-sum game narrative as it does in our financial world. All members of the town are creditors and debtors and the trust relationships allow for the most efficient distribution of debt for the market. There are additional mechanisms in blockchain transaction technology that provide for trusted transactions or insured exchanges when necessary. In addition, once tokenized, the assets can be managed in pools with DeFi platforms to monetize excess Value by moving it into its most productive embodiment. It is productive for the economy to capitalize assets, and when the assets are committed to investment and loan pools this is possible. The dependable and secure and trustless blockchain technologies which can automate these tasks are what make this possible now.

The risk of waiting to build an Information Currency by waiting to capitalize our entities is to continue to irrationally trust a failed language of Value.

Jump In! How to Get Started Using Bitcoin

It is time to practice a bit of the technology. It is best to begin your journey with Bitcoin. Create a Wallet. Buy Bitcoin on Cashapp or Crypto.com by downloading the cell phone app, or SwissBorg or Coinbase on a computer. Practice sending the Bitcoin to a different wallet and to a friend. Order a Crypto Debit card. Load Coingecko app on your phone. Practice purchasing a small amount of ETH and Chainlink (LINK) Instructions to follow!

As mentioned, Cashapp https://cash.app, Crypto.com https://crypto.com, and SwissBorg https://swissborg.com are all apps you can use to buy Bitcoin. Coingecko gives you live Value, charts, news, and other information about crypto coins and tokens plus can track a portfolio. Chainlink is an example of a token representing a decentralized network of nodes that provide data and information from off-blockchain sources to on-blockchain smart contracts.

Now, let's begin!

Begin by purchasing a small amount of Bitcoin. You can buy $10–$100 USD just to start. The goal is to become more comfortable with how cryptocurrencies are transacted. In the United States, the easiest app to use to buy Bitcoin is Cashapp, but there are many apps that will work on a phone such as Coinbase, Crypto.com, Uphold, and PayPal. Some apps for holding or trading crypto will require you to verify who you are before using. This may require that you take pictures of your driver's license or take a picture of your face holding your license up as well. These are standard "know your customer" KYC practices. Outside of the United States, Crypto.com or Swissborg work well. Next, create a crypto wallet with Mycelium by loading this app on the phone. You will be given a set of about 12 words to write down. This is the secret access that you need to write down and keep in a safe place. Practice sending your Bitcoin from Cashapp (or from Crypto.com) into the new Mycelium wallet. You do this by copying the (really long) alpha-numeric wallet address in

Mycelium and pasting it into Cashapp. Over the following week, watch the Value of Bitcoin change in comparison to other currencies. At the end of the week, sell some of the Bitcoin back into the cash dollars that you first purchased it with.

If there is a concern for security, or making an error that wipes out your Bitcoin, of the options, Cashapp in particular may be a safe choice. The app does not allow you to hold your private keys, so there is much less risk of human error, and the public addresses used for deposits change almost daily which averts attack. It is also possible to use a VPN app on your phone which makes it more secure, but really the most vulnerabilities are when users voluntarily give their information to a hacker or spammer. Move very small amounts to practice first because it is easy to make mistakes.

The next exercise is to purchase a small amount of ETH. To do this, first buy some more Bitcoin. Send the Bitcoin to Crypto.com (or buy Bitcoin in Crypto.com) and then buy some ETH with your Bitcoins. ETH coin represents the blockchain that enables smart contracts. The app may say "Trade" Bitcoin for ETH. Next on your computer set up a Metamask wallet. A Metamask wallet is also available on the phone by just downloading the app. Move the ETH to your Metamask wallet by copying the ETH destination address in Metamask and then pasting it as a new send-to address in the Crypto.com app. Great! You're in! The Metamask wallet allows you to use ETH easily from your computer.

Next, it is a great idea to order a debit card to use with your Bitcoin wallet. Cashapp, Crypto.com, Uphold (https://uphold.com), and Bitpay (https://bitpay.com) all have great debit card products. After you apply and receive your debit card, it is important to practice using it in a store or for an online purchase. If you have Bitcoin in your wallet that is connected to your debit card, then in these apps you may first need to move the amount of dollars you need to spend onto the card by selling a bit of Bitcoin back into dollars. Some apps do this process automatically. Regardless, it is great to practice.

Generally, the Value of Bitcoin goes up against dollars over time because there is only a fixed supply of Bitcoin. For this reason, it may be more profitable to keep Value in Bitcoin and only transfer to dollars money you need to be spent at that moment. So even if a store does not take Bitcoin, you can just transfer the Bitcoin back into dollars and spend the dollars. If you choose to move large sums of money into Bitcoin it may be a good choice to spread it out over various wallets, use a hardware wallet like Ledger Nano (www.ledger.com), or you can also choose to allow your bank to hold custody of your private keys. The U.S. Comptroller of the Currency has allowed for this.[2] Many other countries do as well.

The next adventure is to practice sending Bitcoin to a friend. You will need them to copy their wallet address and text or e-mail it to you. You can also scan the QR code that represents your friend's wallet. Then when you are ready to send you just copy it then paste the address in for your friend's wallet, enter the amount, then send!

It is helpful to load the CoinGecko dApp (https://coingecko.com), the CoinMarketCap app (https://coinmarketcap.com), or the Bitscreener dApp (https://bitscreener.com) onto your phone so that you can watch the Values of cryptocurrency fluctuate and also keep track of the cryptocurrencies that you have purchased. The app CoinGecko (www.coingecko.com) is great to load to learn about and track prices of all of the altcoin tokens such as Chainlink (LINK), which represents the Chainlink technology plus new tokens that are being traded on the market. Altcoins are essentially any coin other than Bitcoin. Chainlink is an example of an altcoin that offers technology to connect events in the real world to the blockchain; events like changes in prices of tokens! Loading the Bitscreener app will help you track your purchases, sales, and profits including alts like Chainlink network.

Now ready, set, GO!

What Characteristics Must a New Currency Base for Business Have?

A new Information Currency base will name what is capital and map where that capital is, so that the world can regenerate Value with this capitalization.

The Internet brings the market to us, with company websites that manage databases of their offerings to market. The broadest markets that we have experienced are possibly like Amazon or Alibaba, which use formats for many companies' offers by product. But with this format, the user only has access to the companies that have paid for their items to be displayed, and the market site is managed by a centralized Amazon-like company. Alternatively, blockchain technology attains *decentralized* environments. Oracle technology carries, verifies, and secures data from the ground up instead of from siloed companies. Smart contract technology allows for automated interaction based on set ground rules. Finally, the explorers, or search engines built into the blockchain are able to find messages about items that are carried by tokens.

Most people have experienced search engine technology such as Google and Safari and have noticed the advances that allow a user to ask search questions in almost full sentences. The artificial intelligence technology allows the machines to literally learn from every question around the world every day. On some occasions the user can receive search results that satisfy them. The user can also on occasion feel over-whelmed with the mass of options. But the part of search engine tech-nology that is most counterproductive is the search engine bias, old data, and distracting ads.

So, imagine a free market that would be free from business website silos, free from the barrage of ads and unrelated garbage, free from the database cages that may be out of the thought wheelhouse of most Inter-net users. The way that the world gravitates to "top down" organization needs to be torn down and rebuilt to feed from the bottom up. Instead of organizing the markets as entity (business) to category to item, the mar-kets for Information Currency will reorganize from bottom-up as item (or service) to category and lastly, to entity. It is the information about the items (and services) that will become the currency, literally. So the new thinking and the new search engines will link items as words and their corresponding blockchains (industry and category) as sentences and this will form the market—the Information Currency.

The new dot com-like scramble will look more like an identity crisis. Your business name or Internet silo will not matter as much. It will matter to publicly name the specific microeconomic opportunities. What will matter is if you have synthetically represented and named your product, and that it is connected to the appropriate blockchain. Every day you will need to answer the question, "What is available, where at, and at what Value?" The AMMs are trained to speak item "words" that identify tokens on blockchain "sentences" to make transactions for us. This is, of course, a very simplified explanation.

This new information market will regenerate with your found capital. The synthetic, virtual, capitalized information about your products and services is currency.

How to Integrate Information Currency: Scarcity to Abundance

To first step to integrate Information Currency into your business is to change from sales and profit-focus into production mentality because in this new Currency of Information almost everything produced will find its own abundant market.

What business changes would you make if you knew that virtually everything that you produced, and every service that you offered had an instant sale? Business focus would move to production. But to enter the information currency world, then every item produced and every service offered would need a virtual representation of what is available, where, and at what Value.

Once a market offering is tokenized and connected to the related blockchain, a new, advanced AMM would connect the buyer and the smart contracts would execute and close the transaction. If a transaction was not immediately available and the company wanted the product sold instead of stored against their entity identity (assigned to that wallet address), then the AMM could move a representation of the token to pools of similar tokens of similar products (or services) by area. These pools are a type of purgatory where unused assets can be used as collateral for loans in a DeFi structure. It is already a normalized function for AMMs to integrate multiple collateral pools and connect to other AMMs. The 1inch (https://app.1inch.io) exchange was one of the first to execute this strategy.

To integrate Information Currency into a business is to leverage the information about what is available for Market. Business will need to transform a portion of sales staff into blockchain technology staff who will know that what products and services are defined and set on the right blockchain to be sold.

If this seems unimaginable then remember the significant impact of the Internet on business and the massive structural changes that have happened. Some businesses that participated in the shift changed their business models and some who did not went out of business. Even with the amazing Internet, much of the business data is siloed or stored secretly while salesmen spend large budgets traveling to tell the world about their products. Technology is now able to synthetically represent products and services as tokens and can securely transfer their assignment to entities. The technology can search needs by buyers and can affect the transactions with automated contracts. To integrate, this technology would require retraining of staff and transferring staff into the job of tokenization.

An entire business culture of dollar profiteering will shift into balance sheet steering. The reason is that the dollar-style medium of exchange will no longer need to be hoarded hardly at all.

Your Information will be your currency.

What Key Features Do You Need?

The application program interface (API) that will tokenize your business item data for market will need organization by industry related to naming conventions for elemental products and services. It is a perfect time to discuss this subject and organize or choose an industry group to make these decisions.

Tokenization on blockchain most often happens within specialties. For instance, there is a MED token (https://medibloc.org) for medical coding procedures and a Dentacoin token (https://dentacoin.com) that represents dental services. Nexus Mutual (https://nexusmutual.io) tokenizes insurance, and TRAC (https://origintrail.io) or Morpheus Network (https://morpheus.network) tokenizes freight and logistics. Rarible (https://rarible.com) can tokenize items very easily. Almost anything can be tokenized directly on OpenSea (https://opensea.io) or using Immutable X (see https://docs.x.immutable.com). Industries are adopting specific blockchain environments, and then tech companies bridge into specific token projects. The education and connection to blockchain tech is now business critical.

Industries will need to move their standard naming conventions and categorization standards onto the technology. Then companies can organize their product information to these standards with required specificity and then can mint tokens to represent the products.

The key feature needed to tokenize product or service information is to discover industry standard major and minor categories. This can look a lot like a taxonomic rank that is used in biology: kingdom, phylum, class, order, family, genus, and species. The idea is to gradient down within an industry from largest category to smallest, and then finally to the specificity of the exact product or service. Most industries have associations and offer standard classifications. An example of these is used by freight companies when compiling tariffs such as the Harmonized Tariff Schedule.[3] There are also newly styled database architectures such as the Graph database that do not require hierarchy.

Integrating a business into Information Currency technology is a process that may run counter to conventional ideas to silo business offerings on an owned website where the connection to buyers are the keywords planted there. It is beneficial to move away from siloed thinking and into an idea that products and services need to be launched as commodities into a market that will most always be able to absorb them. The market is made by the efficiencies earned in the transformation of Information into a Currency. The market does not need the dollar as the medium. The market does not need a medium at all. The market functions with Information as Currency.

Handling Security Issues

It is the underlying technology of encryption that makes cryptocurrency and blockchain technology so secure. This is *first* one of eight changes in technology that have made Information Currency workable now.

What happened first, and then what changed in technology to suddenly allow the world to use Information as Currency? Most of the technological advances were security issues. We needed service providers to manage and transact Value data without accessing it. This was accomplished with Zero Knowledge Proofs. Technology integrated a type of math that can prove that another statement is true without revealing the information in the statement. This is like fixing the broker problem. The broker needs to supply a material without the customer knowing where it came from. If the supplier is revealed to the customer, then the customer would just buy from the supplier, and this would cut out the broker.

Second, it was necessary to have accounting for transactions that was real-time, unchangeable, trustable, and discoverable. Blockchain technology fixed a security issue by encrypting transactions, transactors, and the transacted in time sequence. Blockchains make permanent records that are discoverable with the correct explorer technology. The combinations of records are permanent histories of sentences spoken all over the world and by whom. These records insure Information capitalization of markets.

Third, information Currency language needed a way to securely and virtually represent Value words. This was possible with the technology to make a token (like a ticket) for any word or concept of Value. The token of Value could then be named, located, and assigned a relative Value number. Most blockchains created after Bitcoin allow for the tokenization of Value words and their assignment to entities. A further extension of the flexibility of token Value "words" is possible with cross-chain technologies such as Polka-Dot (https://polkadot.network) that can translate tokens into multiple blockchains. As industries and cultures migrate to specific blockchains, this cross-chain technology will contribute to the translation of Value and the operation of transactions (communication) between them.

Fortune 500 companies invested heavily in silos for their Enterprise Resource Planning and Customer Resource Management systems. These companies now have the incentive to move their information to the public ETH blockchains because of the security and simultaneous sharing opportunity provided under protocols such as Baseline[4] (developed by Unibright). This is the *fourth* thing that was critical to effecting a high functioning Information Currency as the manufacturing, distribution, and logistics will need to connect with token transactions and share information without compromising their legacy business systems.

The *fifth* change is that now the token names and labels can be searched with the Etherscan explorer (https://etherscan.io) by smart contracts to locate the information to connect transactions for Information Currency.[5] Block explorer technology aims to enhance searches for tokens, transaction histories, and for entities in exciting new ways.

Sixth, the necessary authentication of entity and KYC technology is required to legitimize and secure Information Currency technology. In the creation of virtual representations of real life, it is critical that identities for virtual entities are protected and legitimate. These technologies have advanced to where they are very dependable.

The specific task to validate and secure the transport of data from the real world into the virtual world is the job of oracle technology. Without this technology, the *seventh* function of Information Currency could not be trusted. This function is so important that it is not uncommon for more than one oracle to be used to validate data that is moved "on-chain." For an example, if a business wants to sell Toyota trucks and creates 20 tokens to represent the trucks, an oracle would be used to validate that there are actually 20 Toyota trucks physically parked in the sales lot. Multiple oracles are regularly used to verify data.

The oracle could also be used to validate the entities titled to those 20 trucks. Oracles can originate with human beings who validate on the ground and then digitally sign off on the data. An oracle can act as a sensor that tracks the location of an asset and sends the location data to the blockchain. An oracle can also be an automated process that checks various resources online and then sends the results to the blockchain. So, the ability to validate the real-world information is an important security function for Information Currency and is operational through the technology of oracles.

The cornerstone, and *eighth* component of a functioning Information Currency is the functioning of decentralized exchanges (DEXes). Basically, the DEX allows for any token to be exchanged for any other token within its blockchain network. DEXes are automated and not owned by any one company. It is the decentralized nature of these exchanges that make them secure because many independent nodes, or computers rewarded by mining, validate the transactions (Bitcoin mining is the process of creating new bitcoin by solving a computational puzzle).[6] Token transactions work between blockchains as well and are enabled using synthetic versions of the native token. For example, if an exchange needed to happen between a Bitcoin and an ETH token on the ETH blockchain, then the Bitcoin can dress up or be wrapped like ETH using Ren technology.[7] The cross-chain technologies allow for tokens to move and be transacted between blockchains, which makes it possible to transact in, or "speak" that language of Value fluidly.

Together, these technologies will secure for you and your business the freedom to speak a new language of Value. In this new language, your information is currency, and you are enabled to speak about your Value and about the Value of your business. In this new language of Value, the market will secure your freedom to speak. The market will understand it when you speak your language of Value.

What Information Is Safe to Make Public?

The coast is clear now to tokenize and collateralize the assets that your company has to sell, the assets that your company owns, and the assets that you identify as yours.

The market was a game where companies had to hide behind their company name in their product offerings. Now a company can offer its products without identifying their source at market until the close of the sale. With technology tools that protect the seller and the buyer simultaneously, the seller enters unabashedly and confidently with the rules of the sale built right into the token's smart contract. It is safe now to declare to market what is available, where it is, and at what Value it is available, because no player has to know who owns the asset until the purchase is made or the supplier chooses to publish the information.

In the old method, for instance, where the supplier information was in front, there often existed a conflict of interest between the manufacturer, the distributor, and the retailer. The manufacturer could not be identified as offering a price that was lower than the retailer, or even offer product for sale at all except through distributors. Though this seems like a productive decision in order to maintain distributor customers, it creates inefficiency at market. The retailer might be able in some circumstances to buy more product than a normal distributor's minimum order. The old method of doing business comes from a point of scarcity where the effort required to gain a new customer was expensive and took time so that the focus was to just hold and maintain the existing customers. With new technology the markets will be able to absorb what is put out to the market because of the efficiencies offered. For most products, the time between what is offered for sale and the time of the sale will not be as critical either because the synthetic representation of the token will have asset Value in the financial markets.

In the old method there also was a conflict of interest between the supplier and the various customers, as customer preference was a game to generate loyalty and repeat orders. The game is costly to the general efficiency of economies. Instead of the products being offered to market to the first taker, the supplier would reserve product for the guarantee of an existing customer and this inefficiency had a high cost to the market in general.

In the same way that the dot-com transition broke down the levels and methods of distribution, the tokenization of assets will create massive market efficiencies at the expense of the archaic sales and broker functions of the past. Sales and brokers will need to reorganize into specialties that can provide assistance to buyers and will contribute to the definition of the tokenization of products and services. Website sales will be made on the blockchain instead, and the old company websites will transition to focus on logistics, contract execution, and customer service.

It will be safe, productive, and amazing to launch products and services for sale into an almost endless customer feast. It will no longer work for businesses to give preference to customers lest they lose all of them to competitors. It will no longer be functional to have staff that does not understand token technology. It will not be regular anymore to conceal your information about what you have, where it is, and at what Value it is available, just to market in a silo with your business name on it. Soon you will discover that the published and tokenized information about your products and services will become your profit and will become your balance sheet, and the unpublished business information that you choose not to tokenize will become your business loss. Your tokenized and published information will be your currency.

Protecting and Leveraging Your Assets

Use excess dollars to purchase crypto assets that have a fixed supply like Bitcoin so that Value can be protected and leveraged as needed. Tokenize balance sheet assets and assets for sale including services defined as available in time. Use the asset tokens for Value validation to leverage new opportunities beyond bank loans. Tokenize assets to

protect ownership rights so that you and your business can be more secure than ever before in history.

First, if business or personal Value is kept in dollars then there is a downside risk as the dollars may be less valuable every day. An option to protect Value is to use excess dollars to purchase Bitcoin. Historically, since its beginning, for more than 90 percent of days, Bitcoin gained in Value over the USD. If dollars are needed, the dollars required can always be sold back from Bitcoin into dollars any second of any day, anytime.

Second, crypto assets can also be used as financial instruments. To explain, the ETH asset can be sent to various crypto finance platforms and used as security for a loan up to 70 percent. These DeFi platforms incentivize token holders to invest and stake their ETH into the platform for a nice return on investment, and then the platform can lend the ETH out. The platforms are decentralized, meaning that they are operated using automated contract technology (smart contracts). The contracts are run by rules in the system and there is no central business entity. For a specific example, it is possible to take $1,000 of excess cash and instead of lodging it in a savings account, purchase $1,000 in ETH. The benefit of the ETH asset is that it typically holds Value or rises in Value as compared to the dollar. Then if some cash is needed it is possible to sell it or to still own the ETH asset but take a $500 loan against it. Any individual or any company can do it. DeFi platforms such as Nexo (www.nexo.io) and Celsius (www.celcius.network) allow a person or a business to leverage excess cash into a crypto asset to earn interest at 11 percent, 20 percent, and even 80% API or use it as leverage for loans.[8] Other tokens are used to leverage Value in a similar way. If the tokens are not already heavily capitalized like stable coins are, then they can be placed in pools of similar tokens to be leveraged as markets become available.

Third, personal and business assets can be leveraged in crypto token form. A tokenized representation of a physical asset or a defined service *will have* a much higher ability to be leveraged for loans or for sales than a representation of that physical asset on a balance sheet for a bank, a representation of the asset on a siloed company website, or even a listing of that asset on a platform like Amazon or Alibaba. The question of when this will be true in your industry or in your country will vary, but the technology to leverage what is tokenized has already outpaced the ability for the financial industry to leverage what is not (tokenized).

Fourth, the way that the blockchain protects assets that you tokenize (again, meaning the assets that you create a synthetic representation of) is by creating an unchangeable record of events related to the asset-backed token. For example, if a property is tokenized, then every transaction related to the property is permanently recorded on the blockchain. A local government could attempt to change a paper record of property ownership (deed), but this would be much more difficult if the property had been tokenized on the blockchain. Industries are moving their records onto this immutable technology to protect and to leverage their assets for growth.

Blockchain technology is how the language of Value is written and permanently recorded.

Company, Executive, and Employee Security Training

The biggest threat to crypto security is a lack of education and a lack of technology practice by employees and company executives.

Security training begins with training on what is Valuable! Crypto coins represent Value of a blockchain (such as Bitcoin and ETH) and tokens represent the Value of other assets created on the blockchain (such as Chainlink, Band, or whatever token that you might create to represent an asset). Think of blockchain as the Value sentence and tokens like the Value words. This Value is designed to be stored in digital wallets. The wallets are like online banking except that the security is significantly better. The wallets are enabled to send coins and tokens directly to other wallets. There is no need for a bank.

By far the most secure storage for crypto wallet private keys (the secret numbers and letters that represent your wallet) and secret seed words or seed phrases for crypto wallets are on paper (a seed phrase, seed recovery phrase, or backup seed phrase is a list of words which store all the information needed to recover Bitcoin or other token funds on-chain).[9] It is good to have two copies on paper in two strategic locations known by two individuals. Though hardware wallets are promoted as secure, they are physical devices. Companies need to know to never communicate private keys or seed words in a picture, an e-mail, or a text—not ever. Some wallets and crypto banks custody the keys for you. This can be good, but the risk and financial independence is then transferred to another.

Almost every crypto user has experienced losing the keys or losing the crypto by sending it to a wallet that does not exist. This is the biggest threat to crypto security! For this reason, it is not enough to simply train company staff on a procedure to handle the company's crypto holdings. The staff needs to practice on small accounts that hold small amounts of crypto. The staff needs to practice with mobile wallets and computer wallets and with exchanges, and in sending and receiving ETH and Bitcoin. This is minimum training. It is about practice.

The crypto education basics include understanding the difference between different blockchains: Bitcoin, ETH, Cardano, Solana, Avalanche, and Polkadot. It is important to learn each use case. Bitcoin is digital gold that is easy to hold, sell, or to buy with dollars. ETH is the main first layer blockchain that has enabled the creation of smart contracts and the transaction base for most of the tokens in the world to date. Cardano (https://cardano.org) is a layer one blockchain like ETH whose founders ruminated in its own creation by insisting on a solid peer-review based build. As Investopedia agrees, what distinguishes Cardano from other blockchain platforms is its commitment to peer-reviewed scientific research as building blocks for updates to its platform.[10] Solana (https://solana.com) and Avalanche (https://avax.network) boast speed and low transaction fees which have been proven in the crypto-gaming sector and will be super important as more companies tokenize their assets. Finally, Polkadot (https://polkadot.network) as a blockchain ecosystem focused on cross-chain interaction between blockchains and tokens. This is hardly an exhaustive list of powerful blockchains.

Then there are stable coins. Stablecoins represent a known Value language and their tokens typically represent one USD, or another dollar language in Value. This is needed for a Value language transition. These would include Tether and USDC. Stable coins such as DAI and XDai are coins that provide a Value with minimal fluctuation. The stablecoins are used often to keep Value ready and secured for trade in crypto form. Stablecoins can also be used in smart contracts to settle on Value. In addition, these coins are used in DeFi to transition entry and exit out of business contracts or investment pools.[11]

CHAPTER 5

Information Currency Applications for Business

Learning From Barter

How Information Functions as a Currency: Lessons in Barter

Lessons in manual barter illustrate how it will feel when physical assets and services transact after being synthetically represented with the new language using token technology on blockchains transacted through decentralized exchange mechanisms.

Information can operate as a currency in a simple, informal barter (trade) transaction between people, or directly by a corporation or government. Examples of manual barter are when a restaurant provides dinner to a customer who washes dishes, when a sign company trades a sign to a lighting showroom for new florescent lights for its manufacturing area, and when a British shoe manufacturer trades a container of shoes for Russian vodka. It does not matter what base of Value that the trade is denominated in, euros or dollars; the fact is that the trades above were not in euros or dollars. The trades above operated with information as a currency. The specific information in these trades included what was available for trade, where it is located, and at what relative Value.

It took more than 10 years for the retail barter and trade industry to move most of the specific information about trade capital available by their customers to an Internet platform. The information about what was available for trade was typically accessible exclusively to members of the trade exchanges themselves. Some trade exchanges began to group together their available trade capital. The companies that built software specifically for trade exchanges encouraged cooperation among their trade exchanges so that the opportunities were bigger for all. The International Reciprocal Trade Association (IRTA), a nonprofit organization, was designed to provide just and equitable standards of reciprocal trade and to raise the Value of reciprocal trade to businesses and countries worldwide (https://irta.com). In 2019, IRTA reported that $14 billion of Value were transacted in trade. This was an early form of Information Currency.

The barter and trade industry practiced an early form of Information Currency by defining the assets of their clients. Barter professionals taught their clients how to quantify their asset offerings to market. For instance, restaurants were instructed how to break down their offerings into tickets called "scrip." In this example, "scrip" would be a ticket for a meal worth $10. For a dentist, service "scrip" would be a ticket for teeth cleaning worth $100. Clients that had product assets were encouraged to define their products with pictures and a price, and then to post them with their location on the barter website that was organized to search by product and by service. But the most valuable contribution of the barter industry is the consultation offered by the professionals to the clients on how to rethink Value in terms of their assets instead of in the language of dollars. The barter industry introduced a language of Value that is about asset things and services and their relationship to the client's business needs.

The barter industry effectively launched listings for the assets available for trade by their customers, but the exchanges still transacted using a medium of exchange by issuing their own currencies called "trade dollars." In the earlier example of the old Western town, the wheat farmer could trade wheat for chickens and intuitively know the relative Value of each. In the town, there was no need for a medium of exchange like "trade dollars." Part of the reason that the barter industry leaned on a "trade dollar" medium of exchange is that most of the assets traded were excess production from external markets. The barter industry marketplace was not complete like the old West town. The exchanges had few commodity type items as assets in the system and so transactions were not as fluid, and it was impossible to intuit relative Value like in the Western town. Specifically, there were few assets for trade in the barter world that all the participants use and know the Value of in common. An example of this is when commodity type items such as groceries, building materials, or toilet paper were introduced into the exchange, these items were hoarded, and the Values bid up way higher than their market Value. Because of this, the exchanges were often imbalanced, and assets offered for trade were not priced relative to market. More than 20 years ago, the top brass at IRTA declared that one of their top industry issues was Valuation. The "trade dollar" medium of exchange has not worked as a Value solution.

If Information Currency is to reach the next level and operate without a medium of exchange, like the trade dollars issued by the barter exchanges, we will need to solve the interim Value challenge. To accomplish this, we can integrate a Value standard based on commodity type items and then assign relative Value to the other items that are not commodities. The Value standard to compare assets can be a basket of needed goods as compared to those same goods in different countries. By comparing that Value basket, we have a base to compare the other products in each economy. This is the function of the Item Banc Index (https://itembancindex.io).

Now that we have blockchain technology with cryptographic account security, we will begin to move forward and assign assets directly to entities to enable exchange without a medium between them. If the entity is a business, then the services available and assets stocked can be quantified and tokenized on a public blockchain. The token representation of a physical asset, for example, can be easily moved directly from one entity (business) to another entity (business). The token that represents the physical asset would not have to exchange into a medium like dollars as it moved seamlessly from one business to another.

Information Currency is operating in some form today all over the world, and even in your city. These lessons learned from the barter industry show how Information Currency functions now and can evolve to dissolve the concept of the need for a medium of exchange (the dollar or the trade dollar) for most transactions in the future.

We now have the building blocks for an Information Currency. They include:

- A structure for Information Currency that has access to a basis for commodity Value information such as BHN, combined with
- Information Currency definitions for tangible assets and professional consulting as functioning in the barter industry, with
- Asset tokenization, exchange and entity assignments made possible with blockchain technology.

Why Fortune 500 Companies Barter

Sixty percent of Fortune 500 companies barter because the language of the dollar does not have Value words to describe excess and non-productive stock. One option to manage these mis-Valued assets is for companies to find specialists who speak the dollar-taboo language called liquidation. A more profitable option has been to engage barter trade consultants. The function of barter consultants is included in the language of Information Currency; to speak of what is available, where it is, and at what Value.

In addition to losing Value, the dollar language fails to inform markets about what is available and where. But is this not the job of salespeople or advertising?

If one chose to drive a truck, would you say, "Is this not the job of horses?" If one sends an e-mail, is this not the job of the post office? Should we not use a global positioning system (GPS) to instruct us because this is what printed maps do? The dollar technology of money is old. New currency technology does more. Information Currency technology informs about what is available, where it is located, in addition to *at what relative Value* it is available. How this works is that the process of tokenizing includes defining the physical asset or service and how many (the *what*), *where* it is located, and its Value. A token in this case is just information about a real item or service projected into a technology form that can be stored, assigned, Valued, and monetized.

Barter is much more like Information Currency because it is about asset things and services with Value that is relative to what else is offered in that barter market. To barter, you must provide the What and Where information. Information Currency uses this same What and Where information, except the information is globally published, military-grade secured, and sufficiently identified.

As users of Information Currency, we will initially face new Value language challenges when transitioning from the dollar. One challenge will be to learn some new technology. Also, in order to speak Information Currency fluently, it will be strategic to absorb methods and thinking that are very much like learning to barter. Why is this so? Because when you dissolve the medium of exchange what remain in the game are the players (the entities) and the asset-things (the tokens). To review, each entity has a digital representation with a total Value based on the assets (tokens) assigned. From that total, an entity can leverage credit to buy. The tokens that represent the Information that defines the real-world assets are simply traded between entities. This is the barter-trade language of Value where Information about the assets *is* the currency.

Barter provides a historical grounding for the new Value language enabled by world-altering blockchain technology. We are reminded of this history by the Guilds of Brussels in Belgium; the Cotton Exchange building in Savannah, Georgia; Sahara Salt trade routes from Ancient Africa; and the Silk Road from ancient China. World economies were built on barter exchange and it is time to resurrect this dependable economic tradition by using the best technology for trade ever available to the world.

The Value Problem

The essence of Value is best learned in the practice of barter.

To get a new concept of Value using barter, you need to experience freedom from the dollar Value language problem. When a customer pays a company for its products with a medium of exchange like the dollar, the Values of a product are translated through that medium. By using the dollar to measure its product Value, a business is forced to carry an external impact such as inflation from central bank currency printing, as discussed. Built into dollar currencies are also market pressures by the irrelevant supply and demand of other products or services that may be overvalued by irrational market exuberance or a supply chain malfunction. A dollar currency can also be undervalued by a trade imbalance or a marketing gap. Barter can circumvent these types of dollar issues.

If a company could pay for all its expenses, including payroll with barter, then the Value of the company's products and services would be magnified. For example, a company can increase and secure its customer base if a business can make a transaction that includes exchanging their product or service directly for a product or service. This way there is less interference and a more direct dependency between the customer and the business. For example, if the business is a restaurant that trades with a printer for its menus, then the printer owners will have more incentive to choose to eat at the restaurant that earns them more printing. In addition, the printer may be more likely to overlook a situation where the dining is more expensive than other alternatives, thus resulting in a more secure customer for the restaurant who traded. Value language spoken directly between supplier and customer can be a method for business to secure a customer base and can also increase their purchases. This type of efficiency will be produced by the automated barter-type technology of Information Currency.

It is possible to pay employees more Value and increase sales with barter. For instance, when a company is no longer forced to sell its products for dollars, it can circumvent the losses of external Value manipulation. A company can pay Value to employees with its own products or services. This is a sale and a payable in the same transaction and leaves more on the table for the employees. For an example, if a company that could not afford additional employees with dollars, it might be able to afford to pay new employees with product. A shoe store could pay an employee in shoes, and the employee could sell or trade the shoes for his needs. The direct Value of employee health benefits, free cafeteria and coffee, and bonus vacations are all in a Value language that is more direct than the dollar and better for a business bottom line than if the equivalent benefits were paid in dollars. These examples are showing how Value is measured in the product or service and not using the language of dollars. Information Currency technology implements more connections and balance in the market.

A company can make former expenses become sales by selling to the same company it buys from. This information about Value without dollar language in the middle can increase sales and decrease expenses simultaneously. In short, if a company can itemize its pre-allocated cash expenditures, then work to trade its products or services for those specific expenditure items then the company can improve its bottom line. For example, a computer distributor who needs to buy billboard advertising can exchange some computers or systems consulting for the advertising. The currency language in this example is the information about the distributor company's product. This is a critical point—it is information about Value given to the billboard advertising company. The

Information Currency language speaks directly about the relative Value of the advertising to computers and services. If each company's payable was a separate barter deal, then a company would need a barter division. But blockchain-based technologies can enable and can automate these transactions when the assets traded are tokenized. Not only does tokenization enable these new technologies to keep up with and secure the transactions, tokenization enables the communication of the new Value language: the relative Value of assets for trades. This is how Information Currency functions.

Bartering, using similar functions as Information Currency, can bring a company an extended set of credit. A company can take its inventory or services and use them as collateral to pay for expenses or assets that are needed now. For instance, if a restaurant needs construction, then it can contract for the work to be done now with an agreement to pay tokens (such as tickets) for meals for later. Another company can commit a set of future services, production, receivables, or existing inventories in exchange for credit that can pay a lease on a building, or for a new truck. This information about specific Value transforms into capital for credit when it is committed to by companies in a barter contract.

When Value information is turned into new Value words (tokenized), then credit can be issued against that collateral using an automated blockchain contract. As an analogy to speech, a speaker can't speak of something that is not defined by a word. An asset cannot be transacted in an Information Currency language unless it is defined by a token. The blockchain can secure Value using automated rules called a smart contract. What this means for an economy is that current and future assets can be assigned credit (Value) without a banking institution deriving interest from, or interfering with, the transaction. Value has always existed in these present and future assets in many civilizations before us and was directly transacted with barter. Now the technology can transform the raw Information into Currency and it is only now, in this generation, ready to be a reality.

Barter thinking makes it possible to understand the bare bones of Value economics, so it is good to review some scenarios to understand the implementation of Information Currency in your own life or company.

Some Basic Tenets of Barter

A company can experience the bare bones of Value when forced to barter for all of its expenses. In this experience, a company would discover a few basic tenets.

The first tenet is that hard-goods chase soft-goods. This means that *physical things* often carry greater demand in barter because the *Value information is more widely known*, or standard. A business typically discovers that it has more confidence trading for a physical item that lasts than for a service or intangible offering. The service may not be delivered, or it may not be delivered well, or it may not be Valued fairly. This intrinsic risk makes the intangible trade have less demand than trade offers for physical items. For example, if a business could trade excess product for a computer worth $500 or accounting services worth $500, most likely it would more often choose the physical computer. One reason that the computer might be the preferred choice is because the information about its Value is tangible and more widely experienced.

In another example, if a lighting fixture distributor had a choice to trade $10,000 in fixtures for $10,000 in certificates toward legal work, or for $10,000 in new flooring for their offices most likely they would choose the hard-good (the flooring). In this case, the flooring has a more predictable Value standard like a commodity standard than attorney fees. The lack of information about a standard Value for the legal work is one reason it is literally less in demand for barter.

In these examples of barter, an item or service is more Valuable for trade if the information about its relative Value is known and has established a standard. In barter economics, the information about Value creates Value. Value information creates liquidity in barter.

Second, that liquidity in barter is universally achieved with the most *basic human needs*. These include food, shelter, clothing, paper products, and hygiene/medical products.

The liquidity of the products and services offered in barter is critical to their Value. Unlike a national currency deemed legal for payment for everything, barter transactions need information about relative Value. Widely used products or services with known Value information make them the most liquid items to barter. The most widely used products that most often have a known relative Value within a community are needed items such as food, building materials, paper products, and basic hygiene/medical items. These are the most liquid items and have the most dependable Value information. Standard items in these categories are the easiest to barter. Based on this truth, we can see the importance of these items to derive the relative Value of one barter economy to another, in general. Consider how easy it would be for a general store which carries most of these standard items, to barter with any business or person in a community! Compare this to how hard it would be for a boat dealer or a painter to barter with every person or business in a community like that.

Our dollar language is eroding. By understanding barter economics, we can lift the Value veil. If we understand the Value bones, then we can understand how to use an Information Currency language to achieve a most rewarding world.

How to Make Contemporary Corporate Barter Work for Our Future

Corporate barter contracts work when a company assigns a set of inventories or services in contract for a corresponding credit Value to spend. This contract design is a blueprint for how Information Currency works for corporations.

The barter industry traditionally focuses on excess inventories that are the signature of where dollars fail markets. The corporate side of the barter industry developed trade contract structures that are a very useful blueprint for the application of Information Currency technologies. First, it is important to review the major components of successful corporate barter contracts, and then look at how this model works with new technologies going forward.

Some examples where a contract applies include: A company has $10,000 in nonproductive inventories that have not sold in the last 12 months. For one such company, a distributor of hardware and lumber, this could be $10,000 in *lighting fixtures* that the manufacturer has to replace with new styles of fixtures. For another company, this could be a restaurant that has $10,000 of food cost in frozen *chicken legs* that company managers no longer want on the menu. For another company, a specialty home care services company, this could be $10,000 of *in-home care* services available by a new care partner's offering. For a delivery company, this could be an under-used delivery route that is capable of $10,000 of more *deliveries* within a month.

With these examples, a market maker contract would be written for a Value in $10,000 of lighting fixtures, frozen chicken, in-home care services, or for deliveries. The contracts for these nonproductive inventories would state that the company that owns the inventories (the market maker) commits them in exchange for a Value of $10,000 of other items or services. Typically, there is a time frame like three years allowed for the market maker to spend down that $10,000 in Value. This is imbedded into the contract plus a guarantee that the items or services traded as payback will have some proof of market Value. The contracts typically make various items and services available to the maker to spend down the contract over the three years. After three years, or whatever time frame for spend was contracted, the transactions are finished, and the contract is over whether or not the original market maker has spent it all or even any of it.

The Role of the Barter Consultant

The role of the barter consultant is to initially make the owner quantify nonproductive inventories, then the consultant contracts with the owner to offer these inventories for barter, then to further define the inventories or services in the contract. After the contract is executed, then the consultant works with the newly contracted market maker to discover what items or services the maker needs. The building supply maker executives might advise the consultant that they need a new forklift and some delivery services. The barter consultant then advises the maker client of what is already available to spend down the $10,000 of trade on. A good consultant would then seek out a distributor or manufacturer of forklifts who had excess inventories and contract their inventories in order to completely fulfill the building supply maker-client. The delivery service would also be strategically offered.

Practice Working in a New Value Language

This barter contract process is a good way for a company to practice working in a new Value language. It is important to identify what assets are not productive in a company. It is also important to set a Value for the assets that are not productive, as the dollar has not set an appropriate Value for the market, or they would be sold.

New technology as has been described in this book will allow a company to contract inventories and services in a way similar to the barter contract—but completely automated. The first part of the contract would be written by creating a token that represents the inventories or services. These inventories can be represented by a token in whole or could be shared (represented in parts). Instead of requiring a barter consultant to sell the newly contracted inventories or services, the smart contract technology makes publishing of the contracted items automatic as the tokens are broadcasted to the world. The token representing the inventory can be automated as well by designating automated market maker technology in the token contract. In fact, the sale of the inventory is of little concern to the market maker, who can use an option to stake (commit) the Value of the tokens to the decentralized finance market as leverage in a pool of tokens for up to $10,000 in Value (as in this example) toward the purchase of other tokenized assets at market from other market makers. The market maker will find an unending supply of options for spending as the tokenization of assets scale around the world.

The contemporary corporate barter industry developed a way to speak a unique Value language for nonproductive stocks using manual contracts for makers who can provide asset liquidity to markets. These contracts bring to life disregarded and dead stock inventories. The success of the barter industry is an early predictor of the vast success to come in a world that has the technology to speak a new Value language. Just like a form of Information Currency is used in barter methods to allow the world to translate nonproductive inventories and services, new blockchain technologies allow Information Currency to Value all corporate assets, not just nonproductive ones. Validated also by ancient methods of barter exchange, we can now build a more reliable technology-based Value language with confidence.

Case Studies in Barter

The following studies are important to understand because barter methods are a precursor to the new Value language of Information Currency that can operate on the blockchain.

How Marriot Executives Solved Their Cash Flow Problem

The story of how the hotel chain traded its rooms for Pepsi machines to save cash

A favorite story that circulated in the barter industry happened in the year 1992. That year Marriot had a severe cash flow problem and asked its supplier Coke (the Coca-Cola Company) to help. Marriot asked Coke if it would consider letting their salespeople stay exclusively at Marriot hotels around the world in lieu of cash payments for Coke machine services and supplies. The story was that the conservative executives at Coke refused the Marriot trade offer. Less than a week after that, Marriot had replaced every single Coke machine with a Pepsi machine at its resorts all over the world! Pepsi accepted Marriot's barter deal to achieve an amazing increase in sales! So, Coke lost Marriot as a client because Pepsi took the trade offer that Coke did not. This story shows what is possible if a company can view its product as payment.

Recently the Coca-Cola Company has been a leader in implementing blockchain technology using Baseline Protocol (which will be explained a bit later in the book).

How the Japanese Captured a Product for Their Market

This is a story about how a nation captured another country's production by trading Toyotas for coffee.

White Toyota cars are all over the Island of Jamaica. This is so because the Japanese engineered a contract to trade their cars for an ongoing supply of Jamaican coffee. This barter-trade deal for the Jamaican Blue Mountain coffee (the finest coffee in the world) is an example of how to use product as currency in the market as a powerful alternative to using dollars.

Ruffin Trading Company Research

Ten years of research proved that dollar failure can be recovered using barter methods that specify information about what is available, where it is, and at what relative Value.

Dollar failure exists when items and services are not selling. The dollar as an intermediary can prevent Value information from getting to market. All items and services find markets with information about what is available, where it is, and at what Value. If there is not a market, then the goods should be in the trash can and the services should no longer be offered. But the proof that the dollar has failed in a specific micro market can be realized if the same goods or services that are not selling can be sold into a separate economy.

The Ruffin Trading Company researched how building materials that were not selling (had zero-dollar Value in sales over 12 months) in the United States could regain Value in a different market. Items were identified as not productive in multiple building supply companies and locations based on stock status reports that showed zero sales in a year. In one instance, over a million dollars of such nonproductive inventory was removed from a building supply distributor in South Carolina and moved to immediately recover its Value in a nearby state.

In a longer-term project, Ruffin took nonproductive inventories—from various building supply companies in South Carolina, Georgia, and Florida—and moved them to a distributor in Montego Bay, Jamaica, where the products were able to recover Value after an average of three months.

Ruffin also proved how excess tile (with zero-dollar Value) in France could be traded for new Value in the United States and Jamaica. Ruffin established these and many other trade bridges to prove that nonproductive inventories from environments of dollar failure could regain Value in new economies using barter methods.

See details in the Appendix, and in the book, *Information Currency: The New Green*, by Virginia Robertson.[1]

Barter Starter: First Focus on Misplaced Values

How to clean up dollar failures with barter methods?

There is a market for everything. When products do not sell it often is that the dollar has failed. The first mission is to discover the dollar failure (things that are not selling) in your business. Consider that the dollar has failed when items in your business are not selling. This is not a conventional statement. Though there are a myriad of potential reasons that the offerings of a business do not sell, in a market with information as a currency all products will find a buyer, or the products will end up in the trash can.

Print an inventory report of what has not sold in the last 12 months. For instance, a building supply business may have 20 pallets of shingles at $1,000 and 10 bunks of plywood worth $600 each for a total of $26,000. Walk through and account for what is not selling and what is not being used. It is important to discover the misplaced Values of space and assets. If your business is service based, then the misplaced Value and dollar failures will be uncovered in areas such as unscheduled service times, meals not served to capacity, routes not run, or rooms not rented. A hotel, for instance, can calculate the lost Value of rooms per month using average room rate of $100, for instance, times the number of rooms not rented over that month, say 30, to get a total of $3,000 per month of nonproductive room inventory. It is important to uncover the misplaced Values of time and capacity because they represent lost opportunities.

The next mission is to send what is damaged, what is in the way, and whatever should be written off to the trash market (throw it away).

After the discovery of dollar failures (space, assets, time, and capacity that have not sold or are not being used), it is really important to quantify each, as in the above examples, to find a total Value.

Each failure needs a count and a Value assignment that matches current market. For example, review your inventory reports to see what items have not sold in a year. Add the quantity of items, multiply by their market price and look at the total Value. If it is a service business, consider the availability for services not used, such as for a hotel, rooms not rented, for a restaurant, meals at capacity not served.

When you have arrived at a total Value in dollars do this first: think of this Value as a dollar failure. This is so because once the markets operate with Information Currency, they will absorb all of production (unless it belongs in the trash). When all assets and services, and when time and capacities are represented by and published in the form of tokens, the markets will find them.

The point of this first mission is to realize and quantify the dollar failure and opportunities lost in your company so that the path is cleared to work toward the amazing potential of the new Value language.

CHAPTER 6

Five First Steps Toward Information Currency

Now you are ready to take your first steps toward using Information Currency in your business.

There are five key steps:

1. Buy crypto and create wallets.

   Get crypto wallets for your company and staff

   The author of this book is not a financial advisor, and this is not financial advice.

   The market will move with or without your business. It is advantageous to learn and it is necessary to acquire cryptocurrencies in order to function in the space. On these accounts, it is useful to invest a portion of cash reserve into Bitcoin and Ethereum. Once purchased, some can be secured in a wallet where the business can retain the public and private keys. A crypto wallet works like online banking except it is capable of not just reporting balances and transactions, it can also send crypto directly to another person's wallet. For business use, a portion of Ethereum can be moved into a Metamask wallet for business functioning on the Internet.

   Web3 (or Web 3.0) means an Internet of networks that are open (built from open-source software), trustless (participants interact without a trusted third party), and permissionless (anyone can participate without permission from any governing body).[1] Metamask (a software cryptocurrency wallet used to interact with the Ethereum blockchain; see www.metamask.io) is deeply integrated into Web3 technology and is a staple for functioning with crypto. Bitcoin needs to go in a different type of wallet and may be most practically purchased and used in CashApp, Uphold, Crypto.com, or Swissborg.

The crypto wallets such as Crypto.com can also issue special Visa or Mastercard debit cards to the business which provides an opportunity to convert the crypto to cash to spend at any point necessary.

2. Add merchant services for Crypto

Be sure to add merchant services for your business that can process crypto payments.

In the same way that businesses need to process credit cards, it is important to clear the path to process crypto payments. Utrust (https://utrust.com) has had great reviews for smaller business. Coinbase Commerce (https://commerce.coinbase.com) works with the popular Poynt systems (point of sale systems). BitPay (https://bitpay.com) out of Atlanta, Georgia, has been a fixture in the crypto world as well.

3. Earn interest or take a loan against your Crypto

Practice leveraging your crypto assets for a loan, or achieve interest in excess of 20 percent annual percentage rate (APR).

A portion of company crypto assets can be moved to a crypto "bank" account such as Nexo (www.nexo.io), BlockFi (https://blockfi.com), or Celsius (www.celsius.network). Interest can be earned on crypto assets and in case business cash is needed, a loan is available up to 50 percent of the Value of the crypto deposited.

The function of decentralized finance (DeFi) can be operated without a bank. This method allows for defined independence and total control over loans and investments, given the required expertise within the business. DeFi protocols use automated systems (smart contracts) to affect a stake (commitment) of crypto assets to a pool (group of similar crypto assets) used to lend for profit. Almost every imaginable financial instrument, including derivatives, are available and automated in the DeFi space. Returns on staking (investing crypto) can exceed 25 percent APR. Staking is available as an easy selection in some wallets such as Argent (www.argent.xyz) or Crypto.com and is also available to select on DEXES such as Uniswap (www.uniswap.org) for token exchange. Some free apps such as the Yield app will work on your mobile device and it finds the best rates for staking (to earn interest) for you.

4. Analyze your business and tokenize your assets and services

Find out the best use for your business specialty on the blockchain.

The first step to discover how the blockchain is directly functional for your business is to learn of the decentralized applications (dApps) that are already created for your business specialty. A dApp is one where there is no centralized company operating the function as it is built to be automated and validated by nodes on the blockchain. For instance, if your business requires logistics, then Origin Trail (www.OriginTrail.io) or Morpheus Network (https://morpheus.network/) may be relevant. If your company needs insurance, then possibly Nexus Mutual (https://nexusmutual.io/) may be relevant. If your business is in Africa, then dApps such as Celo (https://cello.org) and blockchains like Cardano may be the best focus for you. These integrate well with related payment networks or local projects. If you manage real estate, then Aave (https://aave.com/), as partnered with RealT (https://realt.co), may be the best choice to tokenize holdings. A consultant in crypto can help this direction.

To interpret your business Value into Information Currency language, it is critical to tokenize your assets. Tokens come in different forms based on the blockchains on which they reside. The most common token, the ERC20 style, is native to the Ethereum blockchain. This type of token is set up for businesses that have a same, recurring service, or the same, recurring, identical product, as each token is the same as another (fungible). For instance, if a hotel has a standard room, then it could be represented by an ERC20 token where each token has the same Value and represents the same product. If a manufacturer makes standard cans of beans, then all the cans are the same and pallets of the bean cans could be represented by an ERC20 token. If the token represents a specific one-of-a-kind item, or needs to be tracked as such, then an appropriate token form on the Ethereum blockchain would be an ERC721 token, or in cases of a limited set of unique items, the ERC1155 format. This kind of token structure is a nonfungible token (NFT), which means it is designed to represent unique items. It might be a choice by an artist for a unique work of art, or by a construction company that builds homes, for example, so that each home could be represented by a specific and unique token for each house.

NFTs can be easily created on OpenSea (https://opensea.io), in Rarible (https://rarible.com/) and the Mintable (https://blog.mint-able.app/) platform, which advertises that a token can be created on their platform in 30 seconds. Blockchain platforms such as Unibright (https://unibright.io/) integrate legacy systems and also integrate NFT minting.

ERC20 tokens are best created by blockchain developers. This is equivalent to hiring a website developer. Every company needs to contract with a blockchain developer or have one on staff. In a similar way to how business methods moved to the Internet, now it is important to consider how your business can leverage the benefits of permanent transactions and decentralized functionality.

New tools are available for all developers to transition into blockchain technology. For instance, by using the Moralis Web3 operating system and developer environment (https://moralis.io), serverless dApps can quickly be built to model your business methods.

5. Train and reassign staff

Train related staff in blockchain technologies.

We cannot leave our people behind! Training in blockchain and cryptocurrency is critical for company staff and executives. The new language of Value cannot be sequestered in the tech support staff. Accounting staff need to understand how cryptocurrencies work, how they are reported for taxes, and how they should be safely stored and transferred. The staff cannot just attend a seminar. This Value language needs to be spoken and practiced within the company in order to prepare to communicate with the world. Sales staff need to redirect a portion of their time into defining and tokenizing products and services for the business. Executives must understand Information Currency and its implications to keep their businesses moving. This book will provide a good introduction to the paradigm shift ahead of them.

How to Measure Success?

Successful integration of a new Value language into your business requires naming every entity and creating a Value word for every asset by tokenizing each one for the market.

Quantitative Measures

Your business information is currency when all assets offered to market are quantified and then tokenized.

The total token Value issued by the business with inventories to sell should equal the total on their stock status report. For a hotel, the total token Value issued monthly should equal the monthly capacity of the hotel. For a restaurant, the total token Value issued monthly should equal the serving capacity in a month, on average. For a manufacturer, total token Values at market should equal total production. What is not tokenized is lost opportunity to be sold. Tokens that can no longer be used such as hotel rooms represented by tokens that were not rented should be burned (destroyed).

Qualitative Measures

The quality of the tokenized assets of a business relate directly to the relational and identifying information supplied.

How would you communicate if you did not have identifying information such as a name, a phone number, or an e-mail address? Your business cannot "speak" or communicate the language of Value in the form of Information Currency if you do not first set up your business to function on the blockchain. The most basic requirement is a wallet. Where the wallet becomes your digital identity to operate in the decentralized world in which you and your business are able to be sovereign over your Value.

Business asset tokens (words) need to be spoken properly in a Value sentence within a context that buyers can relate to. The token words are about What is available, Where it is, and at What Value. What asset the token represents in the real world needs to be clear, categorized, and connected.

The token description needs to read clearly with the most general description first, and then descend into specifics, such as "Soda, Can, cola, Coke brand, 12oz … ." The token needs to be categorized properly into industry-standard nomenclature and assigned to relevant pools, as discussed in a later chapter. Last, and only last (very different than old school website thinking) is your company branding. Tokens also may need location information down to address. The token must have a price assigned, at least as a beginning offering.

Quality tokenization is well-defined Information about What is available, Where it is, and at What Value.

Estimating a Return on Investment ROI

What is tokenized is sold. The "spoken token" makes this Information a Currency.

The return on investment for tokenizing a business is the capacity for sales total minus the cost for the tokenizing process, and the cost for related education, minus prior year sales. A business will not lose its existing business and only stands to gain by tokenizing.

For example, business assets and services that do not sell immediately at market can be moved into DeFi pools of similar assets and be used as leverage.

Other Important Issues

Train on DeFi Applications

Basic DeFi is a functional engine that provides a crypto reward of Value, such as an APR interest or additional tokens for staking for moving tokens out of your wallet to a specified wallet managed by the automated DeFi application. Most crypto wallet apps allow for a decision to stake the tokens in it for a reward of interest. The Crypto.com wallet, for instance, provides rewards for staking. The Argent wallet has deep options for staking as well. Training on DeFi is done by doing.

Network With Other Crypto Users

Connect to crypto talk on Reddit, Telegram, and Twitter.

Know When Not to Use Crypto

It is not a good idea to speculate on crypto unless you are an experienced trader and to never invest more than you can afford to lose. Crypto markets are volatile. Bitcoin has managed to demonstrate that it is one of the best performing assets in the world over the long term. Inexperienced investors can be impacted by a temporary 30 percent dip in a bull market by selling out of fear instead of holding the asset through the dip. The volatility of the asset is manageable if you are not in need of the invested funds in the short term (less than a year.)

CHAPTER 7

When Do You Need an Outside Currency Consultant?

Your business may need an outside consultant to bring a new perspective on currency into the business. The first step may be to find a barter consultant. The second step is to formally educate one or two staff persons (who understand the business process of the company) in blockchain technology. After training, these staff then they can decide if the business needs the help of an outside crypto consultant.

Beginning With Barter

Professional barter consulting is one of the best ways to help your business adjust out of dollar Value language and position for the new technologies of money.

Arthur Wagner, the president of Active International—one of the premier corporate barter companies in the world—mentioned to me that he experienced again and again that it takes a year and a half for even a well-educated executive to learn to trade and barter. Our language of Value is the dollar, and it will take time to adjust to using Information as Currency. In the same way that you would learn a language faster if you worked on conversational situations with a fluent person, it is advised that you engage a fluent alternative currency consultant (barter professional) to help your business adjust to thinking outside the dollar. The International Reciprocal Trade Association (IRTA), for example, can suggest a local sales consultant who can work with your business until you are comfortable.

Most barter exchanges will engage your business with one of their expert sales consulting staff for free if you will receive them! Match your business sophistication with the right barter exchange. This will involve shopping various barter companies until you find the right fit.

Corporations that wish to trade in excess of $1 million (U.S. dollar [USD]) need to consult with a corporate barter organization. In most instances, transactions less than that typically function through a retail barter organization. Help is available through IRTA at https://irta.com.

How to Determine When You Need Help

In order to determine whether your business needs an outside consultant it is good to realize that in the big picture this technology is new. As much as your business can transform in it, your business also is entering at a stage where you can transform the technology to fit your business as well. An outside blockchain consultant will understand how to implement the technology generically, but an employee of your business can train in using the blockchain and fit the tech to what you do.

It is really best to train a few of your employees on blockchain technologies through one of the online tech schools such as the IBM certification course (www.ibm.com/training/blockchain) or the Moralis Academy (https://academy.moralis.io). This will enable staff that understands the business to combine their knowledge with the tech. Classes are offered in everything from basic blockchain up to relevant classes for Fortune 500 companies that relate to legacy systems and functional subjects such as logistics.

This training will help the employees to determine whether an outside blockchain consultant is really needed. If so, then quality blockchain consulting can be found with companies such as Consensys (https://consensys.net).

Shopping for a Consultant

Once your business and staff connect to the barter industry and train a few of the staff in a blockchain academy, if the need for a consultant still feels necessary then start shopping! First stop is a LinkedIn

(www.linkedin.com) search for blockchain consultants in your city. Some cities also have a Bitcoin or Blockchain group or association and here you may find some authentic help.

In each blockchain niche, whether it is logistics, real estate, oracle information flows, or simply automated, verified processes, online advice is targeted and free from the support staff of blockchain products within that niche. For instance, advice about fitting blockchain process to logistics is available from Morpheus.network (https://morpheus.network) or OriginTrail (www.OriginTrail.io) for tracking. Real estate–related questions on blockchain implementation can be addressed online straight from the related tech projects such as Harbor (https://harbor.com). Opportunities to sell specialty information using the blockchain and derived from your company could generate questions that can be intelligently addressed by the support crew at Zap (https://zap.org/home) or Streamr (https://streamr.network/). More extensive data stream projects can be directed to Ocean Protocol, or to staff at ChainLink.

Building consulting in house by training staff to discover new technologies may be the best solution at this stage in the blockchain industry. It is possible to bring in trainers on site as well even with the well-known academies such as Moralis.

Background and Experience

In the case that your business does choose to hire a blockchain consultant, the areas of experience should include:

- Certification in Blockchain
- Some practical implementation or involvement in an existing blockchain project in a business
- Basic training in Javascript (a high-level programming language), Node.js (a Javascript runtime environment), and Solidity (an object-oriented programming language for writing smart contracts)
- Experience in training business staff including executives
- Experience in applying blockchain technologies in at least three different environments
- Experience in business for a minimum of five years

Familiarity With Your Industry/Business

It is hard enough to secure a good blockchain consultant for your business. To ask that the consultant understand your business specialty is not as easy to achieve given how new the industry is. The best that a consultant can do is train the trainers in your business on how to learn and adapt to the tech in blockchain as it develops. The general learning and direction from a consultant with the staff in your business is the best investment.

If your business is a Fortune 500 sized one that uses legacy-type business accounting and database software for the supply chain process, then the best route may be to engage a company such as Unibright (https://unibright.io) directly to integrate baseline protocol.

Given a strong budget for blockchain, a consulting engagement with companies such as EMURGO (https://emurgo.io) in Singapore, or Charlotte, NC-based PLECCO (https://plecco.net) can assist. These firms are among over 60 reviewed by Clutch (https://clutch.co), an organization that compares B2B software.

Credentials

Some of the best crypto and blockchain tech consultants are self-taught.

That said, if not self-trained, and then the next best advice would be to make sure the consultant has at least basic Solidity (the language for Ethereum smart contracts), Javascript, html, and node.js (the Javascript used for client/server programs training). Certification in blockchain might only guarantee a surface knowledge and then decisions to integrate parts of your business may not be as informed.

Certification in Blockchain is helpful but again, more important may be a functional understanding of decentralized finance applications, or enough business experience to understand what practical uses of the blockchain are relevant.

Referrals to Satisfied Clients

It is important to confirm that a consultant has left the client satisfied. But what is a satisfied client?

It is not enough to satisfy a client business with blockchain unless some staff has received new training and there is a real use case underway. So, when calling for a referral, this would be the type of satisfaction that matters.

Red Flags

If the consultant is unable to explain how blockchain can make functional sense to you in your business environment, then likely he is a "tech head" and not a real consultant.

The best way to spot red flags like this is to make sure some of your business staff are trained by a legitimate blockchain academy ahead of hiring a consultant.

Working With a Consultant

A blockchain consultant needs to find how to apply the technology to your business. This requires first that you understand the main applications and advantages of the technology. Some of the categories of advantage include:

- An ability to transform assets directly into tokens to leverage a world market
- An ability to transform assets into capital for finance and loans
- Finance that is free and functional without a bank involved
- Freedom to send money directly to any business anywhere in the world any time
- Freedom to secure contracts and validate with trustless technology
- Security in a history of transactions
- Secure flow of business data for sale or for private exchange

So, prior to engaging a blockchain consultant, it is important to identify how these benefits apply to your unique business situation.

Preparation for First Meeting

To prepare for the first meeting with a consultant, take the first steps as outlined to discover and quantify the nonproductive assets in your business. The consultant can use this data to transform these assets into leverage for loans or make them saleable.

Look for patterns in your businesses that are critical to prove or keep a record of. These patterns may work well on the blockchain. Your consultant may be able to enable the military-grade security to guard the order, validity, and transparency of your business patterns.

List for the consultant some areas of information like detail on job components or industry contacts that your business has that your business competitors do not. The consultant may be able to help you make money on that data.

Note for the consultant the kind of product or service tracking that is in place in your business. There are fantastic blockchain products that your consultant can recommend. This will make you feel more in control of your supply chain.

Key Questions to Ask

Inquire about Fees and Specialties.

Generally, fees for blockchain consulting are $50–$100 USD per hour. Specialists can charge over $300 per hour (these rates are for 2022). It is important to ask if there is a free consultation up front. Also, the quote should specify how long and how many hours are included over what frame of time. It is always risky to sign an open-ended consulting contract because this incents the consultant to continue booking time.

In the initial inquiry of the consultant, it is good to ask if he or she can consult the company on HOW to implement blockchain in the business, or if they only consult on an implementation of what you, the business, asks for.

It is advantageous to ask the consultant what exact types of blockchain consulting they have provided clients in the past. Testimonials that the consultant can offer work as well.

Tax Consulting for Cryptocurrency

Cryptocurrencies are taxed as capital gains in the United States and many countries. This means that the Value of an asset when it is transferred into another asset is subtracted from its Value at acquisition to arrive at a gain or loss. After this, the tax reporting requires that the gain or loss be categorized as "short-term" (less than a year) or "long-term" (the asset was held more than a year). It is easier to report these capital gains and losses with the help of inexpensive specialty software such as Taxbit (www.taxbit.com).

As of the tax year 2021, it is required that specifically in the United States, we list the capital gains on the form 8949, then move the summary of this to the 1040 schedule D. Corporations or limited liability companies file similar forms 8949 and schedule D for the 1120 and 1065 forms. Most wallets and exchanges will provide the transaction information at end of year and some, such as Uphold, will even send a detailed 1099-B to you.

The challenge in real life is that to calculate capital gain or loss you will need to know the basis cost of each crypto in each transaction. So, for example if you bought $100 in bitcoin at $60,000 per bitcoin in October, then spent all that bitcoin at Christmas when bitcoin was now $84,000 per bitcoin, then your bitcoin was worth $140 at Christmas and the capital gain was $40. The crypto tax programs make this easier because they can more easily look up Values of crypto by date.

There are countries with zero tax on profit from cryptocurrency transactions! Some of these at the time of writing include Puerto Rico, Portugal, Dubai, Malaysia, Singapore, Switzerland, Bermuda, Costa Rica, Malta, and of course El Salvador, where Bitcoin is legal tender.

For tax purposes, our sovereign Value must be reported in dollar language. Please consult your financial advisor or CPA on this subject, as the writer of this book is not a CPA or a financial advisor and this is not financial advice.

CHAPTER 8

Information Currency Products for Business

Listed by category below are the most current, and in this author's opinion, the most important technologies for Information Currency in 2022:

1. Data Flow
Streamr and Ocean Protocol: Stream, Buy, and Sell your Information

Right within reach at https://streamr.network is an amazing environment where it is possible to channel information and profit from it. This platform literally provides a place to stream information and then sell it for XDATA tokens on a public marketplace (which can be traded for ETH and cashed out in dollars as needed).

What could be streamed for profit? Data from your industry that your company has that others may need to use. This would be things such as customer counts, product sales, production counts, or even live price comparisons.

Chainlink: Secure Your Real-Time Data Flow Value

From the real world to the blockchain, data needs to move securely and be checked for its validity. Prices of stocks from various exchanges need to be reliably transported and verified. This application is so important that any big tech that moves real-world data to the blockchain is only considered reliable if Chainlink (https://chain.link) technologies are integrated with other oracles.

2. Finance

Terra Luna: Stable Token for Finance

The Terra's native Luna token offers a unique type of stability to DeFi that has attracted so far over 18 billion dollars in market cap. This blockchain manages the Terra USD stablecoin TUSD. (https://terra.money)

Aave, Maker: Finance Your Assets and Contract Value

Aave (http://aave.com) is a leader in decentralized finance (DeFi) with over $25 billion in capital pledged to the platform. With the Aave platform it is possible to earn interest on your crypto tokens or take loans.

Maker (https://maker.crypto) produces the alternative stable token called DAI, designed to equal a U.S. dollar, that enables a new rebalancing of Value based on a basket of ETH and dollars.

3. Tokenizing and Rails

ETH: Capitalize Your Business Assets by Tokenizing

The base blockchain protocol ETH has become the highway of crypto and the technology platform for the EVM (Ethereum Virtual Machine) where most crypto capital resides. Even Bitcoin assets can travel on the ETH highway as wrapped Bitcoin. ETH is the base protocol because not only is most of the crypto capital in the world on this chain, but also because it was the original beginnings for executing smart contract technology. This was a technology developed to automate instructions on the blockchain. On the ETH blockchain it is possible to create new crypto token assets by creating new smart contracts which issues them and manages their interaction on the chain automatically.

Cardano: Community and Stable Rails

This blockchain offers strong community and has had validation at every stage of growth from a global network of academics.

Rarible: Easily Create a Token

Rarible (https://rarible.com) allows beginners to create nonfungible tokens (NFT) that represent a single, specific, and distinct asset (ERC-721) or a limited set of distinct assets (ERC-1155).

Immutable X: Best in Show

This ETH layer 2 technology for NFT creation is just out of the gate and with Immutable X mint will make digital economies able to power up quickly. (https://immutable.com)

4. Business Process

Unibright Baseline Protocol: Securely Integrate Business to the World

Baseline protocol is a way to move business information and assets securely on the main ETH blockchain and interact with legacy computer systems applications without revealing a company's internal data. Unibright (https://unibright.io) brought this technology to market as a first mover and is currently being used by larger corporations.

Morpheus.Network: Logistics for Big Business Supply Chain

Morpheus (https://morpheus.network) joins Unibright to manage logistics for monstrous projects like Coke.

Origin Trail: Tracking Technology

If you are a manufacturer or distributor and desire exact tracking on your product sourcing this use of the blockchain may fit like a glove. This organization has worked an uphill battle in the grocery sector to make the regulations handled within the technology. For more information go to https://origintrail.io.

5. Insurance

Nexus and Bridge Mutual: Insure the Automation

One of the biggest objections to using blockchain technologies is a risk of losing data or Value to hackers or smart contract (automated functions) failure. These organizations, Nexus (https://nexusmutual. io) and Bridge Mutual (https://bridgemutual.io), insure against these risks.

Insured.Finance: Insure the Assets

Operating on the Polkadot ecosystem, which interoperates to other block-chains, this provider, called Insured.Finance (https://insured.finance) will make sure that there will not be a loss of assets by hacking or through no fault of your own.

6. Markets: Decentralized Exchanges
For Information Currency to work, it is required that tokens and coins can be automatically exchanged. These Decentralized Exchanges, or DEXES, make this work by incenting the staking, or commitment of tokens to the exchange. The incentive includes interest rates or fee rewards. Automated Market Makers (AMM) work these trades in amazing ways and this technology, combined with AI will make markets for capital and products move at a speed we could never have achieved manually.

Uniswap

Uniswap (https://uniswap.org) is the grandpa of exchange and the branding for the rise of the decentralized exchange.

1inch Exchange

1inch Exchange (https://1inch.exchange) was originally designed for investors with larger assets. This exchange searches other exchanges to find the best deal.

Sushi Swap

Sushiswap (https://sushiswap.org) initially copied the success of Uniswap but now offers a long list of assets to convert at competitive prices.

Paraswap

Paraswap (https://paraswap.io) offers a decentralized token exchange for the Polkadot ecosystem. This is the environment which offers inter-chain operability. Unlike previous networks that operated largely as standalone environments, Polkadot offers interoperability and cross-chain communication. It's a network protocol that allows arbitrary data—not just tokens—to be transferred across blockchains.

Pancake Swap

Pancake Swap (https://exchange.pancakeswap.finance) is based on the Binance chain, one of the largest cryptocurrency exchanges in the world, and made history by combining the centralized functions of the Binance exchange extension to make fees significantly cheaper.

Quick Swap

The Quick Swap exchange (https://quickswap.exchange) uses layer 2 Matic (now Polygon) technology to exchange with fewer fees. Basically, the transactions are less expensive because they are taken off of the ETH blockchain (layer one) for swaps.

Dodo

The Dodo (https://app.dodoex.io) is unique because it functions with the AMM without requiring tokens to be staked as pairs. This means that to stake in the system one does not have to deposit an equal amount of ETH, for instance, with an equal amount of another token, but it is possible to simply stake a token.

Open Sea

Open Sea (https://opensea.io) is considered the dictionary database for NFTs and is the most used hub for exchange and even for creation of NFT assets.

7. Contracts
PAID Network

The automated exchanges are strong technologies but people are behind them and your business may be executing transactions with strangers. What if there is a dispute?

The PAID Network (https://paidnetwork.com) provides for those parties transacting to pay a small fee in case the transaction is not satisfying to the customer; then a group of nonparty-affiliated "nodes" or network members function like a binding arbitration—they listen to the debate between the parties and vote on a decision that the parties agreed would be final.

Bondly

BProtect (BONDProtect) is a form of payment processing that is unique in how it provides payment protection services. This service operates similarly to how a Letter of Credit works in sea freight where instead of a bank operating between the supplier and the customer, the BOND on the blockchain performs that role.

Bondly (https://bondly.finance) also offers NFT services, payment processing, BSWAP for token exchange, a marketplace, and more.

8. Superfast and Affordable Blockchains

As the metaverse and gaming continue to lead development in crypto, new blockchains that can move NFT tokens quickly and cheaply are in high demand. The metaverse operates as a 3D virtual world where you can immerse as a character in that world. This will not only be used for gaming, but soon businesses will represent in this world as well. As businesses tokenize their products and services (primarily in NFT forms), similar demand for cheap and fast token transfer will find center stage and so will the blockchain technologies below who have successfully enticed the gaming industry beyond Polygon for ETH layer 2. The superfast and affordable blockchains will naturally work better in the metaverse architecture.

Solana

(https://solana.com)

Avalanche

(https://avax.network)

Fantom

(https://fantom.foundation)

9. IPFS: The new base for Web3 Internet

The Interplanetary File System (IPFS) is the new decentralized base layer for Web3 Internet. Any computer can host by downloading at https://ipfs. io/#install. With this download any file including pictures can be easily saved (pinned) then transported to the blockchain to represent as NFT's with blockchain technologies such as zkSync (https://mint.zksync.dev/).

CHAPTER 9

Seven Steps for Business to Implement Information Currency

After you have determined exactly how you can use Information Currency in your business' specific situation and industry, there are seven key steps to implementation.

An order of operations includes:

Step 1: Identify yourself with a Named Wallet
Go to https://app.ens.domains to identify yourself by name on the Ethereum (ETH) blockchain.

A wallet address can be relatively private if it is only given out when one wishes to receive funds. But it is helpful to have an account that sounds like you just so the sender can be confident that they are sending to the right person! For a reasonable fee, you can change that long line of letters and numbers that represent your public ETH wallet address to some string that looks more like your name.

Step 2: Identify your Business with a Named Wallet
Go to https://app.ens.domains or https://unstoppabledomains.com to identify your business by name on the ETH blockchain.

For your business, it may be wise to purchase your business name domain for Web 3.0 before you get into a position where you have to buy it from someone else who anticipated your need.

Step 3: Choose your Primary Blockchain
Select the ETH blockchain unless you have time to research alternatives, since migrating to other chains from ETH is not too difficult.

The decision about what blockchain your business assets should primarily reside in is huge. Moving to a different one is possible, and there are cross-chain tools and bridges to assist you in this. However, in the search for the right blockchain, there is a discovery process about how your business needs to leverage blockchain technology, and this is healthy. One way to start is to look for distributed applications (dApps) in the field that you need to discover and figure out which blockchains they are using.

What type of business should put its assets straight on layer one ETH? It may make sense if your transactions are few and large and slow is fine.

ETH layer-two choices such as Matic (now Polygon), Loopring, or XDai may give strong connection to all of the financial assets on the ETH chain without the cost. Layer-two moves the exchange of tokens off of the main ETH chain primarily for speed and cost savings. What this means is that to exchange tokens the tokens must be first moved over a "bridge" onto the layer-two, exchanged in that blockchain environment, then that Value sent back over the "bridge" when needed.

Who should operate their assets on Cardano? The Cardano chain may be a choice if the application needs a low failure security, or complex algorithms. Cardano may be a first choice if your business is located in Africa because the community there is very strong. Gaming or high volume transaction businesses should consider Solana, Fantom, or Avalanche blockchains.

Enterprise operations with multiple dependencies may need to lean on Baseline's Baseledger (https://baseledger.net) to allow plug-ins to almost any chain.

Many options for specialty markets exist and technologies such as Polkadot will assist in connecting us all together in the long run.

These options listed are certainly not comprehensive and it would be fantastic to list them all, but it would take another book.

Step 4: Tokenize your Business Assets and Services

Outline the inventories or services provided and break them down into a minimum quantity or time for sale, and then create tokens to represent What is available, Where it is, and at What Value for businesses with quality definition as outlined earlier.

Depending on the size and scope of the products and services that your business provides, there are best choices for the platform to use. Most businesses will find that NFT technology is the simplest way to tokenize and capitalize their assets and service assets.

If you have a small business and want the simplest function to represent assets with tokens, then Rarible should serve your business well. In this dApp, as soon as you create your token you have an option to display in OpenSea, which is an exchange for NFTs (nonfungible or unique tokens). Rarible gives the choice to make single tokens or multiple tokens that would represent the same asset with an inventory of more than one. Rarible makes the account ownership clear, and if you have created your business Web 3.0 identity then you are good to go.

It is also possible to create NFT tokens directly in OpenSea (https://opensea.io). For developers, the new Immutable X platform (https://immutable.com) offers zero gas fees, instant trades, and marketplace growth potential.

For flexible and powerful asset, representation through nonfungible tokenization with low fees and more serious scaling possibility a simple choice is Mintbase (http://mintbase.io).

Enterprise operations, tech specialties, or business with fungible, or recurring same service or asset representation needs can set up tokenization by hiring a local blockchain developer or a specialty company. Enterprise operations with asset inventories or services that are distinctive can work with the NFT program set up by Unibright.

The realization of NFTs representing real business assets ready for ecommerce is functioning using the eNFT protocol marketplace Splyt (https://splytcore.org). Splyt simplifies the e-commerce supply chain by assigning unique eNFTs (e-commerce NFT) to every inventory item, functioning in a way similar to a global blockchain Stock Keeping Unit (SKU) number.

Step 5: Choose your marketplace or pool or create one

Consider a pool as an industry-specific set of products or services within a desired and functional marketplace (which includes regional area desired as sales areas such as country, province, or cities). This is a very new business method and a pool for your industry may not be founded yet.

Thinking in pools or groupings of assets is required to build the most viable Information Currency.

For example, if your business has inventories in canned corn, then a representation of this asset via a token, and placed in a pool of other canned corn or canned vegetables available for sale would allow markets to find your products in a way very similar to Amazon or Alibaba.

If you have an invoice that can be tokenized as an NFT, then the asset representation of that invoice can be grouped with others for leverage in case a business would like to buy your receivables.

If you have a house to rent, tokenize it!! If you have a restaurant with available meals this month, then tokenize them! Next be sure to move these to a pool where they can be traded and seen by markets that need.

If your industry does not have a pool, then one can be created as a marketplace in Mintbase. Open your marketplace to like-tokens and your currency will grow. However, simply tokenizing your assets and making them available on OpenSea or even to DEXES makes them available to the world for instant exchange.

Step 6: Stake your Tokens

Staking your business tokens means committing the assets to a pool. This is similar to posting products or services for sale on Amazon or Alibaba but is different in that the staking allows for asset Value comparisons with other similar assets to derive comps. Staking also provides the option on some platforms to earn interest or take loans against the Value of your tokenized assets.

Staking your tokenized assets to a pool or a marketplace is not much different on the setup time than advertising on Amazon or ebay. One huge difference is this world is not centralized and your business is not subject to the demands of an outside entity.

The other reality is that even as you stake you still own your assets and have taken an amazing opportunity to capitalize them freely.

Step 7: Use DEXES and Make Market Makers

Once staked within a pool, the tokenized assets can be automatically sold through blockchain-based decentralized token exchanges called DEXES. In addition, automated market makers (AMM) can hunt

other available pools that lack the type of token asset offered by your company and can make a transaction automatically with another pool (basically the AMM can sell the products for you).

The DEXES are like the trade managers but are automated without bias. Combined with special tech AMM technologies along with specialized search engines that will depend on AI search engines, (and sometimes on human, manual help), you can be confident that your assets will find their market.

These technologies are in their infancy but will succeed as soon as businesses step forward and tokenize their assets, find or create relevant marketplace pools, and practice using decentralized exchange tools.

Finally, get ready for the Metaverse where by using cutting-edge technologies like Arcona (www.arcona.io), and Boson Protocol (https://bosonprotocol.io) your business can offer your tokenized assets in a 3-D world that represents our real world, and shoppers, operating as Avatars, can browse your store.

CHAPTER 10

Information Currency Explainer

Making Information About Assets Into Currency

Now businesses can make Information about assets into currency by tokenizing those assets, and in this process, "speak" them into existence in a new Value language.

The tokenized asset is an asset reborn into a virtual representation of Value. Once that Value is Information represented as a virtual token asset, it has its own identity on the blockchain and an assignment to its owner's ID address. This way, assets (in the form of tokens) can be sent directly from one owner ID to another owner ID. Unlike money as we know it, a tokenized asset does not need to pass through a medium of exchange (like the dollar), or through a bank, prior to its assignment to another ID.

Imagine Information about assets that look like stickers, stuck to you or stuck on to your company. Facilitated by the blockchain, those assets can be pulled off by your company's ID and stuck to another company or person's ID and the Value assignments follow.

Another way to see this is to return to the barter economy. As compared to how the barter exchange functions, each provider of goods and services in the barter economy would not need to be listed as a member of the centralized barter group. Instead of top-down thinking like a barter economy where it is the barter group, then the members, then the items offered, with a barter broker who assists, Information Currency works from the bottom-up. With the technology of Information Currency, the Information comes from the bottom-up about what assets and specific services supplied can be found by any company or person in the world. Information Currency can work this way because information is free about What is available, Where it is, and at What Value.

Closer to the bottom-up functioning of Information Currency is something analogous to the functions of Amazon and Alibaba. Any entity can search for an asset on a free search engine such as Google and arrive in the centralized world of Amazon or Alibaba to see the asset choices and prices. But the asset information, the Information Currency, is not free information because it is held captive by these centralized platforms that claim pieces and parts of the Value language even before the asset is sold and transferred to another entity. The owner of the asset, in fact, must allow the asset to be held hostage by the centralized Amazon or Alibaba platforms.

When Information is Currency, Value is spoken freely about What asset is available, Where it is, and at What Value—and this free Information operates when the asset is spoken as a tokenized Value word and released into the economy of the world.

It will be a big revolution. Writer Trinity Montoya, in an article titled "Nonfungible Tokens Could Change the Way We Own Things," recently concluded:

With the world becoming more and more digital NFT's present a very viable solution for tokenizing ownership and property. These tokens allow for real-world assets to be properly digitized and stored while simultaneously keeping them secure, ultimately revolutionizing the compensation, storage, legality, and the security of property.[1]

The Best Embodiment: Industry Pools Determine Relative Value

Relative Value can be discovered by comparing like items (similar tokenized assets). It is reasonable to imagine that the clustering of token pools would function best by industry and by item or service.

Given the tokenization of real-world assets into Value words, their connection by industry can organize them to be easily discovered to join into transactions like words in sentences on the blockchain. The categorization and description of a token becomes the critical identifier that can assist new types of automated market makers (AMM) to find desired tokens to connect transactions. Given that the tokens are meticulously categorized, described, and organized into pools of like tokens, the Information about these assets can be readily located.

By tokenizing and pooling like assets within an industry, using a process of publishing What is available, Where it is, and at What Value, and by mapping relative Values in pools of like items, the assets are capitalized for Information Currency. These methods to organize token asset information make Value discoverable like a dictionary for Value language words. As more similar types of assets can be coalesced together in pools, it will be possible to create better Value comparisons based on formulas that use weighted averages of the pricing of these similar assets for comparison. These methods will allow markets to capture their *relative* market Values for price discovery.

Imagine a pool like a fresh market, where all of the lettuce types are together where it is possible to compare various Romaine or Boston leaf or spinach bunches. Imagine how at the market the fish are all together near the services for fish, like trimming the fins or cleaning or fileting. A pool is a virtual place like a market where the owner of the asset can put it on display with like assets for sale. But instead of paying fees to display the assets, like with Amazon, the owner is paid to display the assets. Not only is it possible to be paid by automated technology to display assets, it will be possible to even take a loan against the tokenized assets assigned to a market-like pool. The information about your tokenized asset, whether it is lettuce, fresh fish, or a fish-cleaning service, is spoken about freely and announced all over the world. If the token can connect to other like tokens in a pool, then it can be easier to access and identify and capitalize.

Token pools of like items build structure into the language of Value. The structure includes identifying, translating, and understanding these tokens as Value words. Tokens that represent and identify assets and their identities in pools will capitalize Information as Currency.

This capitalization can happen when there is Value floor such as Item Banc.

Decentralized Finance Is Information Finance

The core benefit of decentralized finance is that Value is defined and financed directly by the entities that own the assets and services. Traditional finance creates silos of Value and claims the Value while injecting unrelated mediums of exchange (dollars) as parties in the transaction.

The tech of decentralized finance can bootstrap Value Information from tokens about the assets, directly back into the economy using language where Value words (tokens) represent real-world assets that speak Information about What is available, Where it is, and at What relative Value. Automated (smart) contracts for finance can leverage tokenized assets automatically for loans. This is the tech "boot-strap" that is badly needed in a financially flat-lining world. Decentralized finance, using these smart contracts, has already automated almost every existing financial instrument. As we evolve Information into our new Value language, decentralized finance technology will progressively financialize all tokenized assets.

Decentralized Finance often uses Value in "pools" of tokens to open an ecosystem for collateralized lending against the Value in the pools. The token providers (stakers) accumulate interest derived from the loans made against the tokens they have committed (staked) to the pools. As a bonus, the tokens in the pools can function as a base for token inventory exchanges (swaps).

Mainstream decentralized finance pools are set up for coins and tokens like Ethereum and Chainlink. The holders of tokens are incented to deposit them into the pool to accrue interest and profits. The pools also make an environment to collateralize loans. It is possible, for instance, to deposit Ethereum in a pool and take a loan Valued at up to 70 percent of the Value of the collateral deposited. The interest accrued and paid by the borrower compensates the pool investors (stakers).

The additional amazing function of the pools is the opportunity for the exchange (swap) of the tokens staked in the pool. In some pools, this provides an additional profit function for the token stakers. Some AMM work by calculating relative Value of tokens by comparing tokens deposited as pairs, like the pair ETH and LINK. As the percentage of a certain token finds scarcity in the pool, the relative Value of the token is rebalanced by the paired token to maintain the Value of the entire pool. Uniswap and 1inch exchange use this type of AMM function and have been very successful as decentralized exchanges, or DEXES, for swaps on the Ethereum blockchain.

Swaps, staking, and loans are necessary for communicating and moving Value with nonfungible tokens (NFTs) as well. NFTs are unique, like a house, a work of art, or a car (because it has a serial number) and are named NFTs to distinguish from tokens that are interchangeable.

For example, in the near future, a Toyota car dealer could represent its inventories with NFTs and add these (stake them) to a general pool of tokenized new cars. The smart contracts can calculate the collateral Value of the cars using oracles (which supply market information) and can automatically lend to the car dealer, or the dealer could stake them to collect interest. In this same example, a Ford distributor could also contribute to the general new car token pool by staking some Ford cars. Then Tesla might contribute some tokens representing some shiny new red electric cars. In this pool of tokens that represent new cars are tokens for Toyotas, Fords, and Teslas. This would enable the ability to swap Truck NFTs… this looks a lot like barter. Centrifuge (http://centrifuge.io) is one of the projects that focus on moving real-world assets to DeFi.

Stable Coins and CBDCs

Stable coins are intended to represent a known Value language.

There are "stable" crypto coins like Tether (USDT), USDC, TrueUSD, Paxos, and Dai that are designed to represent the Value of the U.S. dollar. Some stable coins, such as USDC, are actually (audited) backed by U.S. dollars by balancing the amount of dollars to the amount represented by the USDC token. Stable coins are often used as a translating language of Value for decentralized finance. Crypto loans, for instance, are often paid out in stable coins. Stable coins can also be useful in pools for swaps as they are divisible, and their Value language of a dollar is familiar.

Central banks are issuing their own digital currencies called Central Bank Digital Currencies (CBDCs) as stable coins to use the benefits of blockchain technology. The People's Bank of China has issued its digital Yuan already. As the world transitions into a new language of Value, stable coins and CBDCs will function as a tech bridge between Information Currency and dollars.

A "stable" coin is not stable as a Value language. The USDC, for instance, represents a Value language that changes as the Central Bank prints more money. The CBDCs will be able to create money and put it directly into the account of any person or business and will not need to move through banks.

The CBDC Babel-type dollars are just improved digital cryptographic representations of the same Greatest Deception. The stable coins, however, do enable Value language conversion, as they enable the transfer of Value in digital form based on a known Value dollar language.

With the functioning of Information Currency, where all assets are tokenized, economies will have less and less need or appetite for dollars or stable coins for liquidity. The process of tokenizing assets results in making those assets liquid and identified with a relative Value to market. After this process, the market may find more accurate information about Value directly through the assets instead of dollars.

NFT to Reality

There is an assumption that underlies the theory of the evolution of Information Currency into full digital representation of physical things, services, and their Values. The assumption is, that it is possible to trust that the relationship between the NFT digital representation of reality is reality (the real physical manifestation of that reality). For example, if there is an NFT that represents a specific house at a specific address and a buyer is buying the token with the expectation that that token represents the house, how does the buyer trust this?

To approach this visually, imagine an octopus with its tentacles dangling down and at the bottom they firmly grip a fish. The octopus head in this example is the NFT and the fish is the physical item or service that the NFT represents. What needs to be discussed are the technologies that are the tentacles. These technologies will allow the evolution where the NFT can securely represent reality. These technologies are the oracles.

Oracles are the technologies that are responsible to send real-world data to the blockchain. The process includes a network of nodes or computers that operate as validators of the data.

A process like this can be illustrated with how data is generated about the current market Value of Bitcoin. The Value of Bitcoin can be determined by the current prices that Bitcoin is sold in the various exchanges. Though arbitragers (those who find the exchange with the lowest price

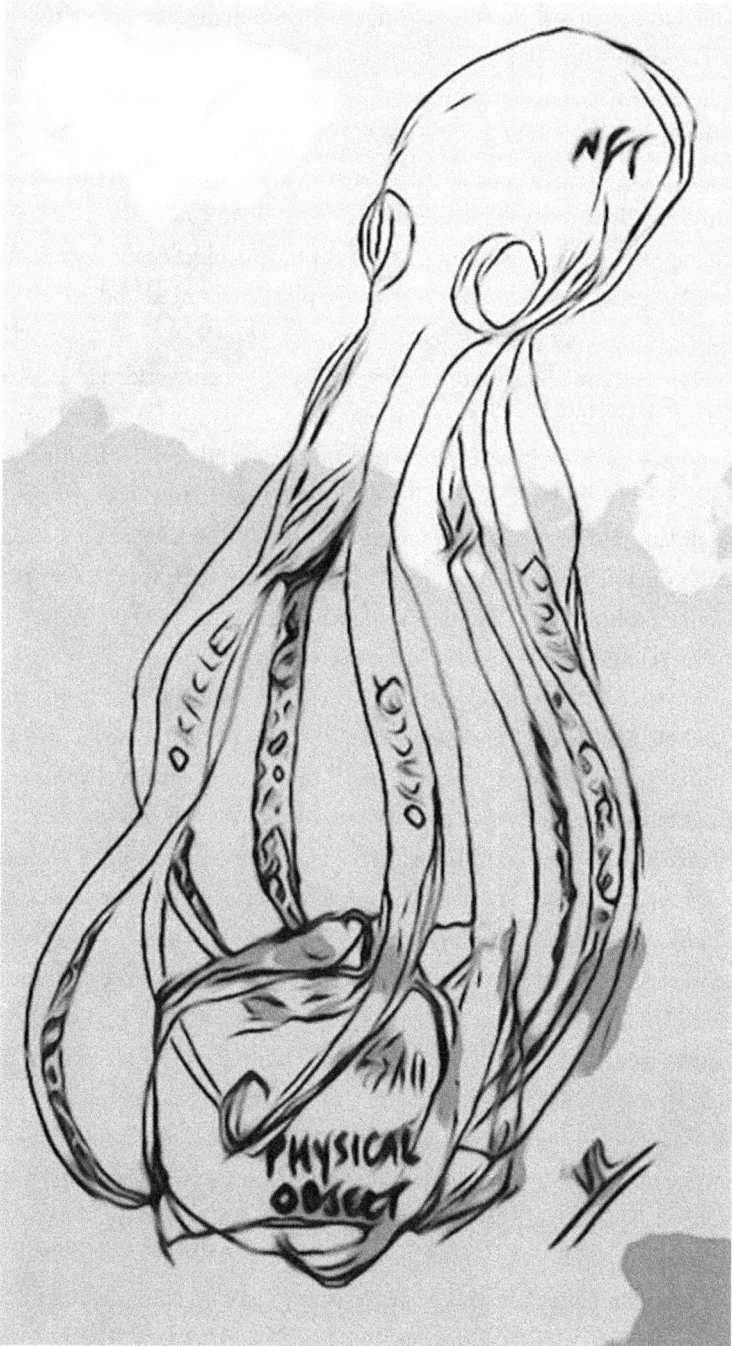

Figure 10.1 NFT octopus (Robertson, 2021)

to buy and then sell on the exchange with the highest price) help keep market Value balanced, the oracles need to constantly read in the data from various exchanges and send this to the blockchain. The dApps on the blockchain then can use their own algorithm to calculate the market Value. What does that mean to send it to the blockchain? The oracles securely deliver the validated data to distributed applications (dApps) using application programming interfaces on the blockchain. For example, dApps such as lending services on the blockchain need updated Value data on Bitcoin and other tokens.

How can the tentacles of oracles work in the real world? How could we achieve sending the current comparables for a house, for instance, that is represented by a digital NFT? How could we validate that the used car represented by an NFT is actually real information? How will we be able to validate that a restaurant that has printed NFT tickets to represent meals available really can produce these? How will we be sure that a ticket represented by an NFT for an NFL football game is not a fake?

Not all of these objections have proven solutions at this time; however, this is where a new industry will build. First, for larger ticket items, this is a whole new field for insurance. Even though the technology of oracles is based on blockchain-interfacing code, this does not mean that human beings cannot be the ultimate validators. A professional home assessor, for instance, can be the first link in the chain to validate the Value of a home, for example, and then the industry-specific oracles can provide additional validation based on comparable data of nearby homes that is available on the internet. The assessor can sign a transaction for Value on the blockchain. The way this works is when the application wants to validate, the assessor would sign-in to the application with their ETH account in their Metamask wallet, for instance, and then the blockchain wallet like Metamask, would send a message to sign, which is a screen with a button that literally says, "sign." This would confirm a permanent transaction on the blockchain including the signed message. Signing messages is one of the most basic functions in blockchain.

Other items such as NFTs representing cars or equipment can be validated by oracles developed within specific industries. The baseline for these has been created already in many industries. Random Lengths, (www.randomlengths.com) for instance, has provided Value information to the lumber industry for many decades. These types of data sources will most likely evolve into the industry oracles of the future.

Item Banc can operate as an oracle protocol for a world baseline on basic human need Values that can enable human validators all over the world by rewarding them with tokens for their work. These "ITEM" tokens can be set up to be used to purchase BHN data entered by others. This process needs to be operated by a decentralized autonomous organization (DAO) to be sure that this most important base Value data is not skewed by a central power. This Value data needs to be delivered from a "trustless" source, which is blockchain-speak for a source that is reliable because it is automated, and the counterparties do not need to trust each other for this reason.

Who are the counterparties involved in the Item Banc oracle? On one side are the people, the consumers who can operate as validators. On the other side are the businesses that supply products and services. This would include organizations that provide financial services and governments.

The need for Item Banc technology can be understood at a very basic level. Almost the entire world realized this need during the Covid years 2019 and 2020. In these years, a most basic question all around the world was about at What basic human needs were available, Where and at What Value. In many cases, it was critical as the prices for basic human needs rose and availability declined. There was a lack of information about where to find basic needs in one's own neighborhood. For instance, during this time, some people in Singapore found out that the prices across the bridge in Malaysia were significantly more affordable and they went in droves to buy in stores there.

With a phone application available that would show the availabilities, location, and prices of basic human needs then people could thrive in a difficult time. It would help suppliers to know where product was needed. It would help governments contribute to supply in difficult times. The head of the United African Blockchain Association sees that this technology would be helpful to many—such as in South Africa (SA) where information about what basic human needs are available at what Value can be critical to survival. An application that allows people to receive this data as a reward simply by entering the quantity and price data they experience in their area could be a relief to many.

Item Bancs by Country: A Proposal for Relative Value Structure

A foundation for the proposed relative Value structure can exist given the existence of the following: a decentralized, autonomous organization (DAO), smart contracts that take in information from Validators about the prices and quantity available of common BHN by country, rewards for these entries with an "ITEM" token, the holder of the tokens to see the current BHN entries in that country.

The ITEM BANC DAO in this embodiment receives basic human need data by country and rewards with the ITEM token, which provides payment for seeing this BHN data by country.

The next building block includes the creation of ITEM BANCS representing each country. These Bancs by country would accept individual basic human need items and prices and available quantities using mobile dApps and would reward the user with a token. This token would deliver information about the basic human need items in that country. If a person in SA wanted to earn an Item Banc SA token, then he or she would enter the price and quantity available of some BHN items in their world. That user would then be able to use the app to see what BHN are available where at what Value in their area, thus providing the critical information needed.

All of the data by country and by item provide a real-time data set that can be used as a building block for a base of Value. The difference is that the data is validated and manifested on the blockchain and is updated in real time. The other difference is specifically the list of basic human need items. This BHN list is designed to identify actual human needs by simulating what items would be needed if a natural disaster happened and what items would need to be put on a container to supply the people in need. From this baseline of Value, calculated by the weighted averages of the availability and prices of the basic needs by country, a baseline of Value can be compared by country, similar to the economic formula for purchasing power parity.

From this baseline, a relative Value structure can be created. Relative Value by country can enable an exchange baseline by country. If the weighted average of the set of basic needed goods is twice as expensive in SA as in the Item Banc of Malawi, then the exchange rate would be 2/1.

This base Value of basic needs would also create an opportunity to understand the Value relationship between other goods and services. In the way that we can relate Value of any item to a national dollar currency as a base of 1, the set of basic needs as a base token 1 could assist in Valuing other tokenized items. For instance, if the weighted average of the basic needed goods has a relationship of 2/1 with the national dollar, then we can understand relative Value of other goods as derived from this baseline in the Value language of basic needs.

Eventually, as national dollars are printed excessively into an economy, the Item Banc BHN baseline information will provide Value security. This baseline will provide structure from which to discover a relative Value to every other item in the economy.

CHAPTER 11

Conclusion

The Entity Revolution

Soon we will be able to direct our Value as Entities.

Human Entities in this world currently function with a Value that is directed by (relative to) the currency of the nation that they are in. For example, a truck driver in the United States is paid in U.S. dollars (USD, the currency of the nation). More specifically, the work of the truck driver in the United States is directly measured in Value by the Value of the USD. When the driver stops at a truck stop for breakfast, he pays in the USD that was earned. If the driver wanted to have his work Valued independent of dollars, then the driver would have to trade his work with the breakfast shop directly. Technology can now enable a human Entity to do exactly that and freely direct their own Value.

The Sovereign Business

New sovereignty can be earned by a business if it tokenizes its assets to direct its Value to the world.

Nations issue and print their own currencies and therefore have sovereignty over their Value. The technology has now arrived that can enable a business to create its own utility currency as well by using new technologies.

A business can define and control its Value directly by launching information about its assets and services as tokens. By taking this action to capitalize business in this way, Value is unleashed, and the business achieves sovereignty over its assets as it is no longer dependent on defining Value by and through fiat dollars. Now a business can be free to directly exchange and monetize its Value. It is no longer required to buy or earn dollars to have defined Value. This means that the truck driver may be able to offer his tokens for breakfast and then drive to deliver that Value. In a "dollar world" the driver would have to earn dollars to then exchange them for breakfast. The dollars that the driver would have to earn may not carry accurate information about the Value of his work, but he is bound in Valuation to the dollar. The driver does not have sovereignty over his Value until his own Value is tokenized, therefore capitalized, and so then represented in a way that can be transacted directly. The international barter industry has proven for decades that it is possible, even without blockchain technology, to define information about capital and execute trades as information currency.

A business can now operate as an independent entity that can self-capitalize by tokenizing its products and services. This is a new opportunity for sovereignty based on the paradigm shift caused by blockchain and smart contract technologies described in this book.

The Sovereign Human

Every human on earth can own his or her own blockchain Entity.

As an Entity on the blockchain, humans can capitalize their Value based on the information regarding their education, their physical assets and acquisitions, their insurance policies, holding of companies, and any other Value information. Just like how almost every company has some presence on the Internet, every physical asset known to humanity will soon be on a blockchain. In the near future these assets will also exist in the Metaverse as a virtual world representation. Your Entity, as an *avatar*, can be as well. But the best part is, unlike social pages where your information is pirated, you will control your Entity and your currency with the most secure encryption ever invented. The Entity of You can store the digital representation of your assets, including some of your own tokens that function like gift cards for your work or services.

Conclusion

If we want to operate independently of fiat dollar language, it is critical to realize our freedom as Entities and subsequently address the question of what our new base of Value should be. If we choose as a Value base the basic needs that we all have as humans; food, building materials, basic clothes, paper products and basic medical/hygiene supplies, then the prices of these items can be compared around the world in every currency. From this comparison, we can generate relative Value information to secure a new base of Value.

Information Currency will be able to function in an ideal form when relative Value systems can compare the proposed base of Value to any currency, to the Value of each entity and to Value sets all over the world. Eventually, systems developers will be able to refine the Value and availability data to connect tokenized capital (that of business production and you and your work) to exactly where it is needed most. Once we achieve this new Value base, then we will achieve Value independence, then businesses and people can discover and own their own Value. This is the Entity revolution.

In this unfolding destination for Information Currency, there will be less dependency on mediums of exchange like dollars. The most progressive and tradable stores of Value will be directly in the assets of people and their businesses. The new sovereign Entities complete Information Currency and we come full circle. We, the Entities, will create this new language of Value so that we, all people, can speak it.

Appendix

Quantifying Efficiencies (Chapter 1)

(see *Information Currency, the New Green*, by Virginia Robertson, 2018, pp. 74–76 accessible at www.ruffintrading.com/InformationCurrency.html)

To analyze the efficiency of transactions that are enabled by barter, there are two sets of Analysis necessary. One study would hold the variable of increased transactions based on Barter. A second study would quantify the efficiencies based on increased or decreased transactions due to a trade/barter environment.

In the first study, we consider the following transactions and compare:

Where Vendor1 = (X) and Vendor2 = (Y),

Transaction 1: "unnatural"

$$X \rightarrow \$Y \text{ and } Y \rightarrow \$X$$

Compares to:

Transaction 2: "natural"

$$X \rightarrow Y \text{ and } Y \rightarrow X$$

(We will explain shortly why one transaction is "natural" and the other "unnatural.")

Transaction one would represent a "dollar based" transaction and transaction two represents an information-based barter transaction. It seems immediately clear that there is an extra coefficient representing the dollar in Transaction one and that there is additional work to get that dollar versus no additional work in Transaction 2.

In an analogy to an island where there are no dollars, imagine the extra work and trade necessary to get them. One can get dollars by exchanging your currency—this could represent a huge loss, and by definition could diminish the Value of your own currency. One could get a loan in dollars and pay an interest rate, or perform inefficient and costly transaction fees to get dollars.

So due to the extra work involved in Transaction 1, we can label this the "unnatural" transaction, and Transaction 2 the "natural" one. For example, when the island without dollars needs computers from a nation with dollars, this may be easy if the nation with dollars needs something that the island makes (bananas, coffee, wood carvings, etc.). If the dollar nation is not able to operate in Transaction 2, then the island would have to then acquire them using very expensive money.

For the island to buy dollars, it needs to trade excess capacity. What if the island does not have excess? Then an interest rate must be paid to borrow dollars. The more scarce (higher in demand) the interest rate is, the higher the rate. It is imperative for the island to keep its trade balanced and find a product to trade out, or a trade "partner" (nation) to buy on behalf of the island nation. The analogies of natural and unnatural transactions with nations can be brought down to a micro level and understood to affect individual transactions using dollars.

In a second study, we can simply look to quantify how many more transactions could occur without the extra work imbedded in the dollar-based transactions. If excess capacity is not spent on inefficient transactions, then they are available to spend on efficient ones. If goods and services are pushed to an efficient place where they will produce more goods and services, then the market can grow. If instead these transactions are spent on interest and extra work, then economies will be forced to cycle based on the starts and stops of banks and governments, the whims of spending based on those who have excess and not need, and the misplacement of Value from the pockets of wealth generated from inefficient markets. These pockets of wealth tend to bid up Value in odd and unproductive places, including the cost of using the dollar.

So what exactly is the coefficient of work to use the dollar? At a microeconomic level, this rate may be represented more as an opportunity cost associated with each dollar-based transaction. A lost opportunity for efficiency is almost impossible to quantify, unless we can speculate that at full efficiency all of us would be rewarded fairly for the work that we contribute to society.

Fractional Reserve Calculation (Chapter 1)

90% of $1000=$900, then that cash loan circulates into another bank that lends 90% of $900=$810, then another loan 90% of $810=$729, then

90% of $729=$656 then 90% of $656.10=$590.49 then

90% of $590.49=$531.44 then 90% of $531.44=$478.29 then

90% of $478.29=$430.46 then 90% of $430.46=$387.41 then

90% of $387.41=$348.67 then 90% of $348.67=$313.80 then

90% of $313.80=$282.42 then 90% of $282.42=$254.18 then

90% of $254.18=$228.76 then 90% of $228.76=$205.88 then

90% of $205.88=$185.29 then 90% of $185.29=$166.76 then

90% of $166.76=$150.09 then 90% of $!50.09=$135.08 then

90% of $135.08=$121.57 then 90% of $121.57=$109.41 then

90% of $109.41=$98.47 then 90% of $98.47=$88.62 then

90% of $88.62=$79.76 then 90% of $79.76=$71.78 then

90% of $71.78=$64.60 then 90% of $64.60=$58.14 then

90% of $58.14=$52.33 then 90% of $52.33=$47.09 then

90% of $47.09=$42.38 then 90% of $42.38=$38.15 then

90% of $38.15=$34.33 then 90% of $34.33=$30.90 then

90% of $30.90=$27.81 then 90% of $27.81=$25.03 then

90% of $25.03=$22.52 then 90% of $22.52=$20.27 then

90% of $20.27=$18.24 then 90% of $18.24=$16.42 then

90% of $16.42=$14.78 then 90% of $14.78=$13.30 then

90% of $13.30=$11.97 then 90% of $11.97=$10.77 then

90% of $10.77=$9.69 then 90% of $9.69=$8.72 then

90% of $8.72=$7.85 then 90% of $7.85=$7.06 then

90% of $7.06=$6.36 then 90% of $6.36=$5.72 then

90% of $5.72=$5.15 then 90% of $5.15=$4.63 then

90% of $4.63=$4.17 then 90% of $4.17=$3.75 then

90% of $3.75=$3.38 then 90% of $3.38=$3.04 then

90% of $3.04=$2.73 then 90% of $2.73=$2.46 then

$90% of $2.46=$2.21 then 90% of $2.21=$1.99…

Exercise (Chapter 2)

Make your own list of about 50 items that you wish would arrive on a steamship container if you had just been through a disaster. Compare your 50 items to the list that follows:

In this exercise, it is important to include food, building materials, clothing, paper products, and hygiene/medical products. These items must be portable (you could pick them up) and must be hard-goods (that can last at least a year), and specific branding is not used.

Basic Human Needs (BHN) for your people—build your example list of items in the five categories:

Paper, Food, Clothing, Building Materials, and Hygiene-Medical

BHN Sample List (Chapter 2)

Paper Products

Toilet paper
Paper towels
Copy paper packages 500 sheets
Paper plates pack 50
Paper cups case pack 1,000
Napkins 1,000/case
Kleenex 85 sheets/box

Food

Can tuna/chicken
Can black beans
Sardines
Peanut butter
Pasta 1 lb. bag
Rice 1.5lb. bags brown
Salt 26 oz.
Coffee instant, 7ct, 49 oz. box
Tea 12 bag box
Can tomatoes
Dried lentils 1 lb. bag
Bottled water 23.6 fl. Oz. (700 ml)
Cooking oil 8.5 fl. oz.
Milk quart box
Milk/orange/apple/veg juice 11.5 oz. can

Clothing/shoes

Sandals/tennis shoes
Socks
Underwear
Jeans/shorts
T-shirts
Sweatshirts
Baby clothes/onesies
Towels and washcloth set
Blankets
Pillows

Medical supplies/Hygeine

Shampoo/soap
First aid kit
Laundry detergent (one load)
Personal hygeine kit (tooth, comb, etc.)
Utensils: fork knife spoon set
Diapers and wipes
Feminine products
Masks

Building Materials/hardware

Plywood sheets 4' × 8' × 3/4", 1/2"
2" × 4" × 8', 12 lumber boards
Tarps 8' × 10'
Metal sheeting 3' × 8'
Quikcrete bags 10 lb.
Hammers and nails and screwdrivers
Flashlights
Swiss army knife
Rebar ½ × 10
Duct Tape 10 yd. roll
Broom

Research: Value Failure of Nonproductive Inventories 2001–2011

Ruffin Trading Company, LLC detailed research on regenerating Value from dead dollar inventories: 10 years, $3.7 million dollars of inventories, 48 U.S. locations, and six countries

Information Currency, The New Green by Virginia Robertson, September, 2018, available at www.ruffintrading.com/InformationCurrency.html

Staking Production for Information

"Contract Samples for Smart Contracts Product for Information Tokens," Item Banc Whitepaper, pp. 32–33, available at https://itembanc.nl/wp-content/uploads/2021/11/Item-Banc-V30.pdf

Item Banc Engine

Item Banc Engine for Conducting Barter Transactions over a Computer Network by Virginia Robertson

U.S. Patent Office, May 1999 (60/132,779), May 2000(09/566,265)

Item Banc Engine Formulas

Tested formulas for Item Banc Index on BHN products

Item Banc Index

Item Index = Sum of Total p*Q / Total Q All Countries

Prices in Local Currencies

	USA	Jamaica	South Africa	Uzbekistan	Haiti	Malawi	Chile	Nigeria	Malaysia	Colombia
Tuna	2	216	16	8000	225	3700	1103	500	6	3800
Tomato	2	421	15	6500	900	1200	2598	270	7	2600
Rice	3	145	11	11500	5100	600	582	1000	6	2300
Soap	1	109	9	1500	285	700	984	200	4	1600
Water	2	60	6	5000	3302	250	621	500	1	1300
Paper	10	903	62	28000	3302	4000	4092	1900	13	6700
Alcohol	2	182	23	5000	2100	1800	1226	350	40	2100
Coffee	10	1456	30	21000	636	1200	2375	1800	28	17500
Tea	5	176	13	6500	320	400	697	900	3	1800
Tpaper	1	74	7	2000	60	500	268	250	1	1900
Sock	3	65	12	5000	600	2500	2682	350	2	3000
Lumber	9	1120	101	10000	1700	12400	7778	1000	31	3900
Plywood	46	6440	570	30000	6460	15000	21456	2900	120	6500
Tshirt	10	140	50	20000	3400	5090	3832	1400	10	14900

	US	Jamaica	South Africa	Uzbekistan	Haiti	Malawi	Chile	Nigeria	Malaysia	Colombia
Basket	106	11507	925	160000	28390	49340	50294	13320	272	69900
Foreign EX to US	1	154	16	10205	98	737	766	381	4	3787
Basket to US	106	75	58	16	290	67	66	35	68	18
Basket to Index	0.007	0.750	0.060	10.434	1.851	3.218	3.280	0.869	0.018	4.558
Index to US	1	109	9	1509	268	465	474	126	3	659

	US	Jamaica	South Africa	Uzbekistan	Haiti	Malawi	Chile	Nigeria	Malaysia	Colombia
Forex US to IndexU	1	30%	45%	85%	-173%	37%	38%	67%	36%	83%

Item Banc Index

Item Index = Sum of Total P*Q / Total Q All Countries

	USA	Pakistan	France	Singapore	Seychelles	Mauritius	Ukraine	Ghana	Kosovo
Tuna	2	1050	2	2	20	25	58	2	200
Tomato	2	80	1	2	32	19	33	2	50
Rice	3	70	2	4	14	44	29	1	60
Soap	1	80	1	1	17	20	17	2	60
Water	2	20	1	1	17	25	8	1	40
Paper	10	1500	3	5	90	100	68	3	150
Alcohol	2	1500	2	8	100	25	39	4	200
Coffee	10	2000	7	7	295	116	164	2	350
Tea	5	100	2	2	30	30	22	2	50
Tpaper	1	50	1	1	7	15	5	1	30
Sock	3	150	4	2	55	35	21	1	60
Lumber	9	7000	4	60	350	900	80	25	200
Plywood	46	10000	9	130	320	1500	160	35	2000
Tshirt	10	2000	8	5	125	100	53	2	1000
	US	Pakistan	France	Singapore	Seychelles	Mauritius	Ukraine	Ghana	Kosovo
Basket	106	25600	47	230	1472	2954	757	83	4450
Foreign EX to US	1	175	0.88	1.36	17.85	39.62	27.6	6	101.64
Basket to US	106	146	53	169	82	75	27	13.83	43.78
Basket to Index	0.007	1.669	0.003	0.015	0.096	0.193	0.049	0.005	0.290
Index to US	1	241.51	0.44	2.17	13.89	27.87	7.14	0.78	41.98
	US	Pakistan	France	Singapore	Seychelles	Mauritius	Ukraine	Ghana	Kosovo
Forex US to IndexU	1	-38%	50%	-60%	22%	30%	74%	87%	59%

Item Banc Index

Item Index = Sum of Total P*Q / Total Q All Countries

	USA	India	Cameroon	Denmark	Turkey	Bahamas	China	Norway	Cyprus	Ethiopia	Poland	Switzerland	Item Index	% Basket	Category
Tuna	2	280	3000	40	29	1	20	13	3	150	5	6	775	5.05%	1
Tomato	2	325	600	4	17	2	40	17	1	65	2	4	545	3.55%	1
Rice	3	20	400	6	24	5	14	23	2	30	2	4	759	4.95%	1
Soap	1	40	300	110	12	1	9	20	1	100	1	1	213	1.39%	5
Water	2	8	150	10	6	1	2	15	1	10	1	1	392	2.55%	1
Paper	10	220	3000	70	79	2	15	239	4	400	9	16	1895	12.36%	2
Alcohol	2	50	500	30	23	9	7	50	2	75	28	4	534	3.48%	5
Coffee	10	190	3000	25	42	5	110	56	10	130	17	8	1813	11.82%	1
Tea	5	140	1000	22	14	1	24	28	3	75	2	4	426	2.78%	1
Tpaper	1	55	300	35	1	3	2	6	1	18	2	1	193	1.26%	2
Sock	3	100	500	20	4	5	3	33	3	50	2	7	527	3.43%	4
Lumber	9	120	1000	143	12	15	100	113	11	180	135	10	1672	10.91%	3
Plywood	46	400	2000	254	15	20	112	149	20	1050	219	9	3720	24.26%	3
Tshirt	10	600	600	300	7	5	41	249	5	300	13	10	1871	12.20%	4

	US	India	Cameroon	Denmark	Turkey	Bahamas	China	Norway	Cyprus	Ethiopia	Poland	Switzerland		
Basket	106	2548	16350	1069	285	75	499	1011	67	2633	438	85	World Index	15,335
Foreign EX to US	1	75.3	567	8.5	9.62	1	6.39	8.73	0.88	47.26	4.18	0.92	Food	30.71%
Basket to US	106	33.84	28.84	125.76	29.63	75.00	78.09	115.81	76.14	55.71	104.78	92.39	Shelter	35.17%
Basket to Index	0.007	0.166	1.066	0.070	0.019	0.005	0.033	0.066	0.004	0.172	0.029	0.006	Clothing	15.63%
Index to US	1	24.04	154.25	10.08	2.69	0.71	4.71	9.54	0.63	24.84	4.13	0.80	Paper	13.62%
	US	India	Cameroon	Denmark	Turkey	Bahamas	China	Norway	Cyprus	Ethiopia	Poland	Switzerland	Hygeine	4.87%
Forex US to IndexU	1	68%	73%	-19%	72%	29%	26%	-9%	28%	47%	1%	13%		

Currency Conversion using Item Banc

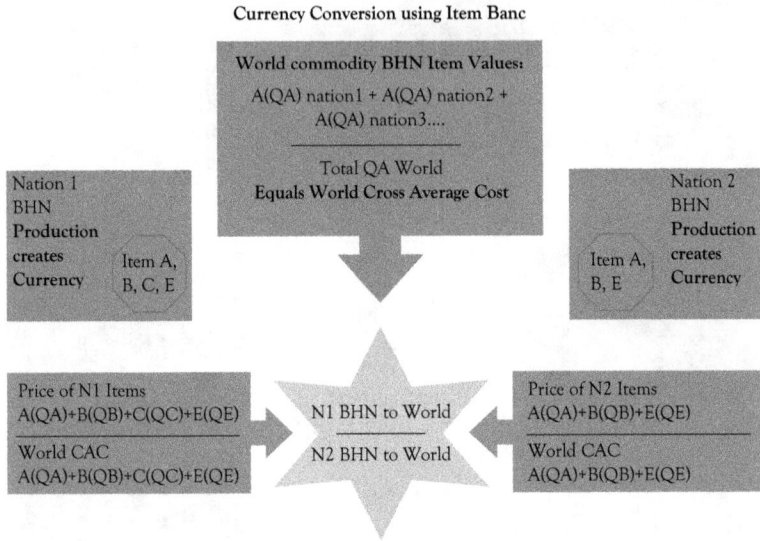

World commodity BHN Item Values:

$A(QA)$ nation1 + $A(QA)$ nation2 + $A(QA)$ nation3....

Total QA World
Equals World Cross Average Cost

Nation 1 BHN Production creates Currency

Item A, B, C, E

Nation 2 BHN Production creates Currency

Item A, B, E

Price of N1 Items
$$\frac{A(QA)+B(QB)+C(QC)+E(QE)}{\text{World CAC } A(QA)+B(QB)+C(QC)+E(QE)}$$

N1 BHN to World
N2 BHN to World

Price of N2 Items
$$\frac{A(QA)+B(QB)+E(QE)}{\text{World CAC } A(QA)+B(QB)+E(QE)}$$

Virginia Robertson, 2020 1.1 Item Banc formulas

Notes

Chapter 1

1. The Analyst Team (n.d.).
2. Bitcoin: Price—https://studio.glassnode.com/metrics?a=BTC&category=&m=market.PriceUsdOhlc
3. The Law of One Price, according to Karl Gunnar Persson, University of Copenhagen
4. www.ig.com/en/glossary-trading-terms/fiat-currency-definition
5. Gethard (n.d.).
6. https://iex.ec
7. https://makerdao.com/en/, https://centrifuge.io/products/tinlake/; and https://aave.com
8. www.swarm-capital.com and https://waves.tech/waves-protocol
9. de Havilland (n.d.).
10. Rouanet (2017).
11. Grant (June 21, 2019).
12. See Max Keiser Reports (n.d.).

Chapter 2

1. For video explanations of liquidity pools, Curve, and Balancer
2. www.coindesk.com/what-is-yearn-finance-yfi-defi-ethereum
3. Garg (n.d.).

Chapter 3

1. www.sap.com/about/company/what-is-sap.html; https://unibright.io/
2. DeSoto (2000).

Chapter 4

1. Bondly is a **trusted, transparent,** and **portable** swap protocol designed to make **you** into a marketplace. See https://morioh.com/p/eccf948083d5. And Paid Network declares itself to be an ecosystem DAPP (decentralized application, a software application that runs on a distributed network)

that leverages blockchain technology to deliver DeFi-powered smart agreements to make business exponentially more efficient; see https://morioh.com/p/25d09bf578a1

2. Pedersen (July 22, 2020).
3. According to Wikipedia, "The **Harmonized Tariff Schedule of the United States (HTSUS)**, also referred to as the **Harmonized Tariff Schedule of the United States Annotated (HTSA)**, is the primary resource for determining tariff (customs duties) classifications for goods imported into the United States. It can also be used in place of Schedule B for classifying goods exported from the United States to foreign countries." The U.S. government provides a search engine for HTSUS at https://hts.usitc.gov
4. Khan (March 08, 2020).
5. You can find the Etherscan explorer search engine.
6. For a more complete discussion of mining.
7. For more information about Ren.
8. For more information about Nexo and Celsius see
9. https://en.bitcoin.it/wiki/Seed_phrase
10. www.investopedia.com/cardano-definition-4683961
11. www.investopedia.com/terms/s/stablecoin.asp

Chapter 5

1. Robertson (2000).

Chapter 6

1. For more information on Web 3.0 see the *Forbes* article.

Chapter 10

1. Montoya (June 28, 2020).

References

According to its website, Bondly is a *trusted, transparent,* and *portable* swap protocol designed to make *you* into a marketplace. See https://morioh.com/p/eccf948083d5 . And Paid Network declares itself to be an ecosystem DAPP (decentralized application, a software application that runs on a distributed network) that leverages blockchain technology to deliver DeFi-powered smart agreements to make business exponentially more efficient; see https://morioh.com/p/25d09bf578a1

Bitcoin: Price https://studio.glassnode.com/metrics?a=BTC&category=&m=market.PriceUsdOhlc

de Havilland, P. n.d. "What is a Blockchain Oracle?" Available at https://cryptobriefing.com/what-is-blockchain-oracle/

DeSoto, H. 2000. *The Mystery of Capital.* Basic Books.

Etherscan Explorer Search Engine at https://etherscan.io

For information about SAP see www.sap.com/about/company/what-is-sap.html. For Information on Unibright see https://unibright.io/

For more information about yearn see www.coindesk.com/what-is-yearn-finance-yfi-defi-ethereum

For more information on Web 3.0 see the *Forbes* article at www.forbes.com/sites/forbestechcouncil/2020/01/06/what-is-web-3-0/?sh=7817b41558df

For more Information see https://iex.ec

For video explanations of liquidity pools, Curve, and Balancer, Available at https://youtu.be/-OVcVC8_TXA and https://youtu.be/bCLJUT3jCm4

Garg, P. n.d. "Chainlink, Band Protocol, API13, and Umbrella Network: Exploring the Differences Between Oracles." Available at https://medium.com/umbrella-network/chainlink-band-protocol-api3-and-umbrella-network-exploring-the-differences-between-oracles-9477d975e142

Gethard, G. n.d. "Falling Giant: A Case Study of AIG." Written for Investopedia.com at www.investopedia.com/articles/economics/09/american-investment-group-aig-bailout.asp

Grant, J. June 21, 2019. "Alexander Hamilton Would Not Approve of Today's Federal Reserve." *Barron's.* www.barrons.com/articles/alexander-hamilton-federal-reserve-51561084647 (accessed May 21, 2021).

http://eh.net/encyclopedia/the-law-of-one-price/

https://en.bitcoin.it/wiki/Seed_phrase

Khan, F. 2020. "What Does the Baseline Protocol Intend to Achieve?" Available at https://medium.com/technicity/what-does-the-baseline-protocol-intend-to-achieve-54c4d93b1efe

Max Keiser Reports; though he is a Bitcoin Maximalist (one who invests in Bitcoin exclusive of any other cryptocurrencies), at www.rt.com/shows/keiser-report/

Montoya, T. June 28, 2020. "Nonfungible Tokens Could Change the Way We Own Things." *Cointelegraph.com*. Available at https://cointelegraph.com/news/nonfungible-tokens-could-change-the-way-we-own-things

Nexo and Celsius see https://decrypt.co/57289/blockfi-celsius-nexo-what-is-the-best-crypto-savings-account and https://bitcompare.net/versus/celsius-vs-nexo

Pedersen, P. July 22, 2020. "OCC Allows Banks to Hold Cryptocurrency Assets for Safekeeping." *American Banker*. www.americanbanker.com/news/occ-allows-banks-to-hold-cryptocurrency-assets-for-safekeeping

Ren see www.kraken.com/en-us/learn/what-is-ren and www.youtube.com/watch?v=Yb4cn10WSIQ

Robertson, V. 2000. *Information Currency: The New Green*.

Rouanet, L. 2017. "How Central Banking Increased Inequality." *Mises Wire* of the Mises Institute, Available at https://mises.org/library/how-central-banking-increased-inequality

See https://makerdao.com/en/, https://centrifuge.io/products/tinlake/, and https://aave.com for more information about these products

See www.swarm-capital.com and https://waves.tech/waves-protocol for more information about these products.

The Analyst Team. n.d. "What Is a Blockchain? Introduction to Digital Ledgers." Available at https://cryptobriefing.com/what-is-a-blockchain-digital-ledger/

Wikipedia. n.d. "The Harmonized Tariff Schedule of the United States (HTSUS), also referred to as the Harmonized Tariff Schedule of the United States Annotated (HTSA), is the primary resource for determining tariff (customs duties) classifications for goods imported into the United States. It can also be used in place of Schedule B for classifying goods exported from the United States to foreign countries." The U.S. government provides a search engine for HTSUS at https://hts.usitc.gov

www.ig.com/en/glossary-trading-terms/fiat-currency-definition

www.investopedia.com/cardano-definition-4683961

www.investopedia.com/terms/b/bitcoin-mining.asp

www.investopedia.com/terms/s/stablecoin.asp

About the Author

Virginia B. Robertson has been the CEO of Ruffin Trading Company, LLC in South Carolina for over 20 years, and is also currently the Director of the startup Item Banc, Inc.

Her training is in Economics and her business experience spans years in systems, international trade, countertrade, wholesale distribution, and corporate barter.

Virginia has been passionate about the development of the technology named Item Banc since 1998, as she believes that one day, Information will be our currency, and it is critical to enable a technology such as Item Banc to determine a base of Value related to basic human needs.

This book achieves her goal to explain how the blockchain-related technologies that are available today solve many business challenges that she personally experienced over years. She believes this book will inspire a vision on how to use blockchain technologies to navigate the sea change ahead in our use of Value language.

Index

OTHER TITLES IN THE ECONOMICS AND PUBLIC POLICY COLLECTION

Jeffrey Edwards, North Carolina A&T State University, Editor

- *Transparency in ESG and the Circular Economy* by Dolan Cristina and Barrero Zalles Diana
- *Developing Sustainable Energy Projects in Emerging Markets* by Francis Ugboma
- *Understanding the Indian Economy from the Post-Reforms of 1991, Volume III* by Shrawan Kumar Singh
- *Understanding Economic Equilibrium* by Mike Shaw, Thomas J. Cunningham, and Rosemary Cunningham
- *Business Liability and Economic Damages, Second Edition* by Scott D. Gilbert
- *Macroeconomics, Third Edition* by David G. Tuerck
- *Negotiation Booster* by Kasia Jagodzinska
- *Mastering the Moneyed Mind, Volume IV* by Christopher Bayer
- *Mastering the Moneyed Mind, Volume III* by Christopher Bayer
- *Mastering the Moneyed Mind, Volume II* by Christopher Bayer
- *Mastering the Moneyed Mind, Volume I* by Christopher Bayer
- *Understanding the Indian Economy from the Post-Reforms of 1991, Volume II* by Shrawan Kumar Singh

Concise and Applied Business Books

The Collection listed above is one of 30 business subject collections that Business Expert Press has grown to make BEP a premiere publisher of print and digital books. Our concise and applied books are for...

- Professionals and Practitioners
- Faculty who adopt our books for courses
- Librarians who know that BEP's Digital Libraries are a unique way to offer students ebooks to download, not restricted with any digital rights management
- Executive Training Course Leaders
- Business Seminar Organizers

Business Expert Press books are for anyone who needs to dig deeper on business ideas, goals, and solutions to everyday problems. Whether one print book, one ebook, or buying a digital library of 110 ebooks, we remain the affordable and smart way to be business smart. For more information, please visit www.businessexpertpress.com, or contact sales@businessexpertpress.com.